WH.
Three Life-Changing Commands of Jesus

"If you believe, as I do, that God is love, it only makes sense that we should do our best to love God, obey Him, and help others deepen their relationship with Him. In *Wholehearted*, Roger Wernette details these three concepts in a way that is interesting and easy to understand. If you want to grow in your faith, you need to read this book."

—KEN BLANCHARD
coauthor of *The One Minute Manager®* and *Lead Like Jesus*

"This book is so simple that all can understand and use it. I like the prayers that I am challenged to pray and I like the goals for my spiritual life. You should read *Wholehearted* and then use it to impact those around you. As this book teaches, love God, obey God, and help others to do the same."

—LANCE BERKMAN
Major League Baseball Player

"Without clear cut goals, you cannot run a successful business. It is also important to have goals for our Christian life as well. *Wholehearted* sets out some clear goals from which we can all benefit. It tells us where we should be heading with God."

—DRAYTON MCLANE
Chairman and CEO, Houston Astros
Chairman, The McLane Group

"I always tried to make my business logical. I wanted all of my people to know our mission and understand what we needed to do next. The Christian life should be simple. Jesus clearly told His followers what they should do. Somewhere down the line, we have made it complicated. Roger brings us back to our roots and I greatly appreciate his effort."

—NORM MILLER
Chairman, Interstate Batteries
author of *Beyond the Norm*
co-founder: I Am Second (www.iamsecond.com)

"A practical approach for turbulent times, *Wholehearted* is a straightforward view of discipleship that will challenge and encourage you to develop the most important relationship you can ever have. Read it. Apply it. Grow!"

—SPENCER TILLMAN
CBS Sports
author of *Scoring in the Red Zone: How to Lead Successfully When the Pressure is On*

"This book speaks to everyone who thirsts. We want to love God more. We want to obey God. But how? Until I read Roger's book, I hadn't really considered where to go to find an answer to these questions. Within his book are simple, yet powerful, steps to take which enable us to draw on the same Spirit who commands us to love, obey and teach."

—LLOYD M. BENTSEN III
Chairman, Houston Christian Foundation

WHOLEHEARTED

WHOLEHEARTED

THREE LIFE-CHANGING COMMANDS OF JESUS

Roger Wernette

Whitecaps Media
Houston

Whitecaps Media
Houston, Texas

whitecapsmedia.com

Wholehearted: Three Life-Changing Commands of Jesus
© 2010 Roger Wernette
All rights reserved

ISBN-13: 978-0-9826353-2-2

Printed in the United States of America

Roger Wernette may be contacted through the publisher

*In memory of my mother, Doris,
and in honor of my father, Fred,
who first taught me to love Jesus*

Contents

Lost & Not Quite Found

Command the Israelites and say to them: "When you
enter Canaan, the land that will be allotted to you as an
inheritance . . ."

—NUMBERS 34:2

LORD, you have assigned me my portion and my cup;
    you have made my lot secure.
The boundary lines have fallen for me in pleasant places;
    surely I have a delightful inheritance.

—PSALM 16:5–6

SOME OF US are lost out here.

When I say we are lost, I mean we have forgotten our
vision and direction. We have become lost as the church of
Jesus Christ, as the body of believers. We each heard about
the gospel: how the Creator of the Universe came to earth,
and how He died and was resurrected in order to bring all
things back to Himself (Colossians 1:20). These truths of
the gospel sounded good to us. We understood our sin and
wanted to repent. We wanted to embrace the One who designed this earth and who made each of us. So we came to
Christ and began to live a brand new life. Yet, somewhere
we misplaced our vision for the life to which we were called.

And some of us want it back! Each of us should know there is more to the Christian life than a decision. We just need someone to put it into simple terms so we can understand. There is no doubt about it. Some of us are lost out here. And you may feel like one of "us."

In the Christian life, I am afraid many of us are traveling without any idea of where we are going or even where we *should* be going. Without a clear-cut vision, our lives become a passionless meandering trail that leads to who-knows-where. What we all should want is a purpose that is so strong it requires a dedicated life. We find meaning in a wholehearted pursuit of a quest that is greater than anything we can imagine. We want a quest that is greater than we are and that takes a lifetime to complete.

At about the age of twelve, I attended vacation Bible school. In East Texas, where I grew up, everyone went to "VBS." One day our pastor visited and gave us a brief sermon. At the end of his talk, he asked us if we wanted to go to heaven or hell. I kind of favored air conditioning, so I raised my hand for heaven and went down front so that Jesus would forgive me of my sins. I was told that once Jesus forgave me, I never had to worry again about hell. I had my ticket punched for eternity. No one ever told me that there was something else to the Christian life. I thought I understood it all. I continued in that thinking all the way through my undergraduate work in college. After receiving a degree in computer science, I decided to get a graduate degree in business. Two years later I set out to make my mark in the world of finance. Still, no one had told me more about the

Christian life; that my decision as a twelve-year-old had only been a start.

I began to look for jobs in Dallas since that is where every red-blooded East Texas boy wanted to live. At the time, there were few opportunities in that city for a computer and finance guy, so I did the unthinkable. I sent letters to some companies in Houston. No one from my town ever wanted to move to Houston. It was too hot and too big. But one night, I actually prayed to God. It was the first time I had ever asked Him a question about my life. My request was this: "Lord, if You have a plan for me and it involves Houston, I will go. I want to do what You want me to do." I did not know it at the time, but that prayer changed my life.

My first interview in Houston was with Pennzoil Company. As I walked in to meet the person who had a job opening, I noted a placard on her desk. It said, "Praise the Lord." Somehow, I knew I was going to work there. Sure enough I did. In fact, that wonderful lady helped me greatly to understand the Christian life.

As the years went by, I wondered what "growing in the Christian life" meant. I would hear someone discuss it, but no one would ever tell me how I could grow or how I could do "the will of God." I soon found myself in the volunteer leader ranks of Young Life, a ministry to high school students. Now I was teaching young people how to grow in their faith, but truth be told I was not exactly sure how to do it myself. I went on the full-time staff of Young Life, and still found that I had much to learn about becoming closer to God. Ten years later, in 1998, while heading up the

Houston ministry of The Gathering of Men, I was coaching men on how to begin and grow in their Christian faith. I realized that the concept of "living with Jesus Christ" was not clear to most men, as it had not been for me for so long. It was out of this process that this book was born.

I get frustrated when I hear others describe their lives as exciting when mine is drab and boring. I want my life to be characterized by a wholehearted desire to achieve whatever it is that God wants for me. I want to be passionate about my Christian life! I do not want to just read about those who have given their life to God's purposes. I want to be one of those people! If my spiritual journey is just about showing up and sitting in a pew, then maybe I want to re-negotiate the deal. If I am just supposed to be good and not drink, smoke, or chew (or hang out with girls who do), then I signed up for the wrong life. But if we are talking about meaning, then that is a different story. Give me a vision that I can sink my teeth in *wholeheartedly*, and I will knock you down getting to it.

Shortly after I graduated from college and started to work, a friend of mine, Steve, convinced me to go to one of those "free" weekends you earn by listening to a real estate pitch. The deal was this: "Come to a weekend at our resort, free of charge, and all you have to do is listen to a sales presentation." Since we were single and in search of adventure, we went. We soon discovered the pitch lasted almost three hours and culminated with our salesman taking us to a piece of land that had been picked especially for whichever one of us turned out to be the lucky buyer. We quickly wished we had just paid for our stay instead of attending the tour.

Arriving at "our" new vacation site, the salesman turned off the car. As we sat there, it became evident we were not leaving until somebody bought something. Since the engine had been shut down, there was no air conditioning. The car soon began to heat up. Beads of sweat accumulated on my forehead. Neither of us had ever experienced a sales pitch like this. We gazed at a wooded area while our determined salesman described what it would look like after the development was complete. We were asked to imagine ourselves vacationing in this "beautiful" spot. Unfortunately for him, we were both recent graduates with no money to spend. We finally were able to refuse his gracious offer to sell us our dream property. Rather than making us walk back to the lodge (which I would have gladly done), he kindly gave us a ride, all the while reminding us that we were missing the deal of a lifetime. How could we be so foolish to pass up this unsurpassable opportunity?

How did we pass it up? It was easy. We had no vision for what the salesman was telling us. We could not imagine that among all those rocks, weeds, and lizards, lay a piece of land that could have been developed into a nice place to live. All we could think of were the problems. First, we had little or no money for the development of the land. Maybe, just maybe, we could have taken all of our savings and made the first payment. We had no motivation to do that. Even if we had purchased the land, we did not have the resources to develop it. So for us, it was not worth what he was asking us to pay. Despite the financial payback promised to us, we just did not think enough of the idea to make the sacrifice. If we had truly believed in what we were being told, maybe we would have scraped by and made the investment. But we didn't. The land lay undeveloped and unclaimed as we drove off.

You and I are getting ready to discuss spiritual growth. Many people are lacking in vision when it comes to the Christian life. We have been told that Jesus died on the cross that we might live forever in heaven. Believe in Jesus and we get to go to heaven when we die. The gospel, as many present it, is more about dying than living. When Christians die, they go to heaven. *But what if we live?* Does the gospel have anything to say to the living? Most of us look at life in the same narrow way my friend and I did when we considered the vacant lot. We do not have much vision for it. We really are not sure what our life purpose should be. But wait, we *do* have a goal. There is hope . . .

Our goal in life is the knowledge of God.

J.I. Packer, in his classic book, *Knowing God*, says the following:

> What were we made for? To know God. What aim should we set ourselves in life? To know God. What is the "eternal life" that Jesus gives? Knowledge of God. "This is life eternal, that they might know thee, the only true God, and Jesus Christ, whom thou has sent" (John 17:3). What is the best thing in life, bringing more joy, delight, and contentment, than anything else? Knowledge of God. "Thus saith the LORD, Let not the wise man glory in his

riches; but let him that glorieth glory in this, that he un-
derstandeth and knoweth me" (Jeremiah 9:23).[1]

Jesus did not live and die and come back to life just so we
wouldn't go to hell! It is certainly the case that Christians do
not go to hell when they die, but there is something much
greater than even this. Jesus came to bring us to God. Our
salvation is not about a destination. It is about a relationship. We begin a journey toward knowing God when Jesus
rescues us from a life estranged from our Creator. The goal
we are given by Jesus is the ability to know God.

Our problem is we are still not sure what to do with
this objective of knowing God. Most of us have no spiritual
goals. We know what we want to accomplish in our business, sport, or education, but have no idea what we would
like to achieve in our life with Jesus Christ. In the world of
commerce, we know we are supposed to make money. We
seek promotions mainly because the "higher-ups" make
more money. What are we to do in our spiritual lives?

I once heard Dr. Howard Hendricks of Dallas Theological Seminary tell the story of a businessman who came to
see him for counseling. The story may summarize our dilemma. The man described his career and talked about the
many successes he had experienced. Since most of us go to
counseling for failure, not success, the man's story did not
seem to add up. As Dr. Hendricks questioned him further,
the real problem came out. The man said, "All my life I have

[1] J.I. Packer, *Knowing God* (InterVarsity Press, Downers Grove,
Illinois, 1973), p. 29.

climbed the ladder of success, yet when I got to the top, I found that the ladder was leaning against the wrong wall." The top of the wall was not what he thought it would be. He found that his success was not satisfying. It was not the driving purpose that God had for him.

For many, the Christian life has become more about achievements than knowing God. I do not need just something else to accomplish. I want *significance*. I want to know what God was thinking when He created me. I yearn for God's best for my life. God must have a place for me, and I want to find it. In order to reach the pinnacle of success as defined by God, I must be sure that my ladder is leaning against the right wall. Do I listen to the allure of the world or do I seek to find real life through a relationship with God? If I seek my answers in God, how will I know what He wants me to do? We only get one life on earth, so the question has huge implications.

The Christian life is a lot like a marriage. Those of us who are married have discovered, to our delight, that the wedding is only the beginning. While the nuptials end, the relationship lasts for a lifetime. In the same way, our life with Christ is not a one-time decision. It is a lifetime journey. God has given you an unbelievable and undeserved chance to get to know Him. Can you imagine that the One who created the universe wants to know you? He has opened up the way for this knowledge to flow to you. When Jesus came to earth, He said, "The kingdom of God is near" (Mark 1:15). It is an invitation for you to draw near to the heart of God. He came to give you a chance to know and have a friendship with the Creator of the Kingdom. Your purpose in life is to grow in this knowledge. J.I. Packer asks the question, "What do I intend to *do* with my knowledge about God, once I have got it?"[2] If we have been given a way to know God, how do we go about it?

What if there were three simple biblical mandates that would allow us to develop our vision in the Christian life? What if they weren't wearisome, but rather enlivening?

The major part of our life with God can be summarized in three great commands. These instructions can be succinctly stated in eleven words. These mandates are fundamental and set the stage for the rest of our life in God's kingdom. God furnished us with these crucial orders that serve to build a foundation to our lives with Him. If we will focus on them, much of our confusion will fade away.

In Mark 12, we find the first directive and the key to our personal relationship with the Creator. Someone asked Jesus what the greatest commandment was. He answered, "Love God with all your heart, soul, mind, and strength." Jesus said to love God with all that you have. Such a simple concept! **Love God.** We need to know and love our Creator. Jesus' Great Commandment calls us to do that. Through that command, Jesus desires to empower us to fully appreciate His identity and His plan for us. If we love God with all our being, the love of other things and people will take

---

[2] Packer, p. 17.

a back seat. The love of this world will no longer hold its spell on us since our top priority will be to love God first and foremost. Our love for God will become the motivation of our lives.

Next, we need to know how to show our love for God. How can one know beyond a doubt that the love of God is a top priority in his or her life? How do we measure love? Jesus said, "If you love me, you will obey what I command" (John 14:23). He *did* leave us a way to measure our love for Him. It is called "obedience"! If we love God, we will want to do what He tells us to do.

This, then, is the second important mandate. He asks for our obedience. **Obey God.** Our love for Him will cause us to do what He tells us. As we come to love God more, we will look for ways to obey Him. We will read our Bibles with new interest. His directives found in Scripture become opportunities for us to become more like Him and to demonstrate our love for Him. As He molds us to be His people, He expects us to use the Bible to discover His commands so we can grow to become what He intends. This mandate gives us evidence of our love for God.

Finally, we should want to know that we have a reason to be in the Kingdom. *Why* did God save ME? If the basic tenets of the Christian faith are true, that is, if Jesus was God come to earth, if He died for our sins, and then rose again from the dead, shouldn't it be for a greater cause than a legalistic conflict of who is the "best Christian"? Seriously, did Jesus come to earth so that we could receive a five-year Sunday school pin? Was the Revelation of the Eternal God through His Son meant to allow us to obey a list of "dos and don'ts"? Or is salvation just about making us comfortable? Did Jesus leave heaven to save us to a life of safety and ease? I do not think so! We need to have an objective in God's kingdom that has eternal implications. We want to *really* count. We all need a mission, and God has given us one that will last eternally.

His third command gives us purpose. The last thing Jesus said when He prepared to ascend back to heaven was recorded in Matthew 28:19–20. If to love and obey God is fundamental to our faith, we should **teach others to love and obey God.** He commanded us to make disciples everywhere. Jesus wanted his followers to carry on the work He had started. He commanded them to make disciples. And what would be better to teach them than to love and obey God? What is more important to impart than those two actions? What is discipleship if it isn't to teach others to love and obey God?

So, here's the hypothesis: To be true to the meaning of the Christian life, which is to know God, we are to:

Love God
Obey God
Teach others (to love and obey God).

We can use the acrostic "LOT" to help us remember our path. A "lot" is one's fortune in life. It can be described as one's fate. It usually carries a negative connotation: "We are stuck with our lot in life." Here, however, it is anything but negative. This lot can serve as a fantastic vision of our spiritual direction. It will point us to our lifelong dream: to know where we came from. To know our Creator. To finally have direction that will guide us in our spiritual journey. When I give my life to this goal, I will find that I will have passion for life. I can be described as "wholehearted."

We start this journey by attempting to master the three major commands discussed briefly above. In the following pages, we will provide insight into the depth of those commands and will leave the reader with some tools to complete this task of living the Christian life.

Here is one brief caveat before you read further. I am not saying that the way to get to God is to simply begin trying to love and obey Him. The only approach to God is through the forgiveness of sins provided by the death of Jesus on the cross. It is only in His sacrifice that we are given the freedom and ability to love God. The empowerment of the Holy Spirit then gives us the desire and ability to love God as He commands. When we fail at that task (note: not "if"), Jesus offers us the grace to continue toward the lot to which He calls us. Our love of God comes only from Him, and we must never forget it. My wholehearted vision is given to me by God. I can't just conjure it up. I must seek it and God must grant me success in the journey.

In the following discussions, I will present three prayers, one for each of the mandates. I hope each of us will be given a growing desire to pray them daily. They are the kind of prayers I believe God will answer because they turn our hearts to Him. As our love for Christ grows, our faith and relationship with God will mature. As we grow stronger in

Him, our drive to obey will increase as will our motivation to make other disciples. Isn't it about time all of us got serious about those things?

Discussion Questions

1. What was your initial experience with faith in Jesus? How has the result of this continued with you?

2. Does the idea of God's "lot" for your life excite or trouble you? Why?

3. When you hear the words "spiritual growth," what comes to your mind?

4. What does the "average Christian" think God wants Christians to do?

5. Would you like to know the will of God? Why or why not?

6. What do you think it means to love God with your whole heart?

Chapter One

Love God

> One of the teachers of the law came and heard them debating. Noticing that Jesus had given them a good answer, he asked him, "Of all the commandments, which is the most important?"
>
> "The most important one" answered Jesus, "is this: 'Hear, O Israel, the Lord our God, the Lord is one. Love the Lord your God with all your heart and with all your soul and with all your mind and with all your strength.' The second is this: 'Love your neighbor as yourself. There is no commandment greater than these.'"
>
> —MARK 12:28–31

THE ROOM WAS crowded and men were pushing to hear the reply of Jesus. They were close, and the air smelled of sweat. For some time, the priests, scribes, Pharisees, Herodians, and Sadducees had tried to convict Jesus of disobeying the law. This group included most of the important religious and political factions in the country. They represented an extremely diverse set of beliefs, yet they all agreed on one thing: Jesus was threatening their lifestyle and prestige. The argument about and with Jesus had continued for some time, and now, maybe now, they had Him. One of the teachers of the law had just asked Jesus, "Of all the commandments, which is the most important?" (Mark 12:28). The teacher asked that question since Jesus had given good answers to several preceding inquiries. Maybe this was his

chance to trap Jesus or maybe to determine if Jesus was who
He said He was.

If Jesus picked out just one of the Ten Commandments,
these teachers could criticize Him, because all the commandments were important. Yet He had to pick at least one
of them, or else He could be accused of evading the question. It looked like Jesus was stuck in a difficult place. How
could He answer correctly? Surely they had Him this time.
Jesus' answer started with the words, "The most important
one is this . . ." Did He hesitate to allow the drama of the
moment to take over? Did everyone stop talking in order to
hear the answer?

How would *you* reply to the question? What *is* the greatest commandment? What *is* the most important task for the
follower of Christ? The question speaks to a basic dilemma
within our faith. As Christians, we are not sure what the
most important issues are. There seem to be many of them.
We need a clear beacon to serve as our focal point. Even in
the church, we are uncertain about our priorities. What is
the number one goal of Christians and of the church? If
you surveyed ten different Christians, you might receive as
many varying answers. Our uncertainty leads us to search
endlessly for effective programs and set goal after goal, typi-
cally resulting in frustration.

Jesus continued, "The most important one is this: 'Hear,
O Israel, the Lord our God, the Lord is one. Love the Lord
your God with all your heart and with all your soul and with
all your mind and with all your strength.'" There was the
answer. It was a passage of Scripture they all had learned

as children and recited all of their lives, Deuteronomy 6:5. How could they forget? It was right there all the time.

This passage, called the *Shema*, was prayed every day, morning and night. It indicated that the obligation to love God stemmed from the uniqueness of God.[1] In a world of many gods, it called on the people to believe in the One True God. God was to be loved by each person for His own sake and uniqueness. Everyone in the room with Jesus that day was familiar with this passage. They knew it, but they were not living it.

How did they forget such a fundamental command? They had allowed their religiosity to replace their love of God. They had become lost in trying to protect their way of life. Their priesthood had become a career to be shielded and preserved. They wanted to play church instead of worshiping the God who had founded the church. These men had developed an ancient fraternity, complete with rules and nuances that actually kept people from knowing the real God. They had substituted legalism for the privilege of a relationship with God.

Jesus' answer was so simple. Go love God. They must have been stunned. "Well said, teacher," the man replied, "You are right in saying that God is one and there is no other but him. To love him with all your heart, with all your understanding and with all your strength, and to love your neighbor as yourself is more important than all burnt

---

[1] William Lane, *The Gospel of Mark* (Eerdman's, Grand Rapids, Michigan, 1974), pp. 432–433.

offerings and sacrifices." The man must have choked out the words, and now he was the one who was stuck. Jesus left him nothing to debate. Jesus' questioner almost certainly had recited those verses from Deuteronomy that very day. Now, all the religious leader could say was, "Well said." By the way, no one asked any more questions. They knew they had been beaten.

Jesus told him, "You are not far from the kingdom of God." The questioner had stumbled upon the heart of the faith. Love God. That is what it is all about. This is what it meant to "not be far from the kingdom." The man was not called to love the rules or love the building or love the leaders of the church. He was simply asked to acknowledge the God who "is" instead of the God that he had invented through his legalism. And then he was called to love the true God with his whole being.

So what does it mean to love God with all our heart and with all our soul and with all our mind and with all our strength—to love God wholeheartedly? It is all encompassing. We are called to love with our heart; that is, our passion. When we give our *heart* to something or someone, we give our dedication and our zeal. The heart refers to our emotions, desires, and passions. Loving God with our *soul* speaks of loving Him with who we are on the inside. We give our soul only to those interests that touch us to our core. We are commanded to love God with our *mind* by exercising it for Him. We learn, we teach, we think. Finally, it will take all of our mental and physical *strength* to love God. It is not a lackadaisical exercise of just believing a few things and showing up at a few places at the right time.

William Lane, professor of biblical studies at Seattle Pacific University, in his commentary on Mark says:

> It is the Lord our God who is to be loved with a completeness of devotion which is defined by the repeated "all." Because the whole man is the object of God's covenant love, God claims the whole man for himself. To love God in the way defined by the great commandment is to seek God for his own sake, to have pleasure in him and to strive impulsively after him. Jesus demands a decision and readiness for God, and for God alone, in an unconditional manner.[2]

Jesus implies that we have to use ourselves up in the task of loving Him. If we are to love God with all our being, we must give all that we have to give. No wonder Paul, at the end of his life, stated he was like a drink offering that had been poured out:

> For I am already being poured out like a drink offering, and the time has come for my departure. I have fought the good fight, I have finished the race, I have kept the faith. Now there is in store for me the crown of righteousness, which the Lord, the righteous Judge, will award to me on that day—and not only to me, but also to all who have longed for his appearing.
>
> —2 TIMOTHY 4:6–8

In true love, there is no holding back. When I get to the finish line, I have used it all. What a total waste to complete a cross-country race and not be tired. It would mean you

---

[2] Lane, p. 432.

didn't give your all. Paul says to Timothy that he had completed his task, he finished his race, he was poured out. What else was there to do? His life was lived totally for God.

I have been a Christian for forty-five years. Most of that time I have to admit I have not done my best in loving God. The world gives me so many things to love: cars, houses, vacations, sports, reputation, and thousands of other things. These interests can captivate me to the point that I forget about God. How can I love God when my television tells me that I have to be rich and that I must love my red convertible? (A Mercedes, if you don't mind. That two-seater, with the tan leather seats.) Even in my ministry, The Gathering of Men, I sometimes have become obsessed with results and have overlooked the real point of my life, which is to know and love God. I started out to know God, but I wind up searching for measurable successes instead.

In the Timothy passage, Paul said his desire was to give it all and to lay it all on the altar. Does that make you feel inadequate? My efforts feel laughable in view of such commitment. How in the world can I ever love God in the way that Jesus commands me? How can I get where Paul was? The things of this world get in the way and I give my heart, soul, mind, and strength to them instead of giving them to God. It seems like Jesus is calling me to an impossible task. It makes many of us want to pack it in and give up. If it cannot be done, why go on?

Before their fall Adam and Eve lived in perfect communion with God. Nothing impeded their love for God. When sin entered their lives, they lost this relationship

and turned to other things for their satisfaction and happiness. The love of earthly things did not, however, satisfy
their need for God's love. In their excellent book, *Longing
for God*, Richard Foster and Gayle Beebe describe our longing for the love of God:

> This problem has plagued us since the Fall. When Adam
> and Eve allowed their passions to overrun their rea-
> son, they set in motion a chain of events that has never
> stopped. Our original relationship to God was based on
> the submission of our will to God's will. When Adam and
> Eve disrupted this order, they sabotaged our natural hu-
> man destiny. And this disordering of our natural destiny
> caused us to lose our sense of God. As a result, we no
> longer seek him.[3]

Peter closes his second letter with the words, "But grow
in the grace and knowledge of our Lord and Savior Jesus
Christ" (2 Peter 3:18). If we want to grow in our knowledge
of God through loving Him, why don't we? As Christians,
we *say* that we want to love God, but in the daily activity of
life, we wind up loving other things instead. We verbally
state that we want one thing, but we live out something entirely differently. Paul laid out the problem in Romans 7:

> I do not understand what I do. For what I want to do I
> do not do, but what I hate I do. And if I do what I do
> not want to do, I agree that the law is good. As it is, it is
> no longer I myself who do it, but it is sin living in me. I

---

[3] Richard J. Foster and Gayle D. Beebe, *Longing for God* (InterVarsity
Press, Downers Grove, Illinois, 2009), pp. 91–99.

> know that nothing good lives in me, that is, in my sinful
> nature. For I have the desire to do what is good, but I can-
> not carry it out. For what I do is not the good I want to
> do; no, the evil I do not want to do—this I keep on doing.
> Now if I do what I do not want to do, it is no longer I who
> do it, but it is sin living in me that does it.
>
> —ROMANS 7:15–20

Obviously, we have a problem. Why would we want to love God but continually choose to love other things? As Paul details above, it is our sin that takes us away from God. Even as Christians, there is a fight going on inside us all the time. The struggle between God's way of life and the world's way collides within us and causes us not to love God as much as we love possessions, position, and power. This is the age-old problem of which Jesus spoke when He told the Pharisees in Luke 16:13–24, "'No servant can serve two masters. Either he will hate the one and love the other, or he will be devoted to the one and despise the other. You cannot serve both God and Money.' The Pharisees, who loved money, heard all this and were sneering at Jesus." These religious leaders had forgotten what their true calling was. They had replaced the love of God with the love of religious practices.

The fact is that we are not that different from the Pharisees. They loved position and power every bit as much as we do. No one likes to be compared to Pharisees, but isn't that the real truth? Aren't we very similar to them? How will we ever love the right thing? Here's the answer to making God our top priority: We need God to draw us back to Him.

We need His empowerment to want Him more. We need greater drive than we currently possess to love the God who created us, who sacrificed for us, and who loved us first. We need Him to change our minds, to bring us back to Him and win us over from the love of things. This sounds like the problem to which Christ is referring in Revelation as He talks to the church of Ephesus:

> You have persevered and have endured hardships for my name, and have not grown weary. Yet I hold this against you: You have forsaken your first love. Remember the height from which you have fallen! Repent and do the things you did at first.
>
> —REVELATION 2:3–4

He explains that while the Ephesians had been diligent in their work and had made it through many difficult trials, they had lost their struggle in trying to love Him. Their sin was not that they had not worked hard; it was that they had not loved God. They had abandoned their first love and forgotten the greatest commandment.

Is that where we are? And if it is, what can we do about it?

We need a change in our lives. We need to be transformed. We need to seek His enabling power to help establish our priorities. Since God created us, He can certainly remake us and alter our lives. If God gives us a command, He will also furnish us with the strength to obey. So let me now remind each of us that there are some wonderful reasons why we should love God. After that reminder, we will then ask God to accomplish this task in our lives.

Discussion Questions

1. If you observed Christians that you know, what would you think is their most important goal?

2. How do you react to Paul's example of being a drink offering?

3. Why do we want to protect our lives? What keeps us from giving it all?

4. What messages from the world (like billboards, television ads, magazines, etc.) cause you personally to measure yourself against others around you?

5. What part of God's love and the gospel is hardest for you to grasp?

Chapter Two

Because He Is Our Creator

In the beginning God created the heavens and the
earth.

—GENESIS 1:1

I believe in God, the Father almighty, creator of heaven
and earth.

—APOSTLES' CREED

HOW DO YOU think the world got here? It is important to
have an opinion. We did not just appear out of thin air. The
way you answer that question will affect how you live your
life. We cannot just shrug our shoulders and believe the
latest sound bite on the ten o'clock news. How can we live
our lives on this earth and not wonder how the universe
came to be, and how man came to hold his place within it?

If you were walking across the desert and found a Rolex
watch in working condition, keeping perfect time, your
first thought would be, "How did this get here?" You would
most likely believe someone left the watch there. You would
not come up with a story that somehow the watch came
together by itself or that it was flying through the air and
landed in the desert. A watch is much too complex just to

"happen." You would tell yourself that someone must have designed and built it, and someone else must have accidentally dropped it at its present location.

We live in a universe that is infinitely more complex than a watch. Scientists spend their whole lives trying to explain and understand even small portions of the human body. Someone might devote years of study to the molecule, the stars, the migratory patterns of geese, or the minerals of the earth. Imagine what processes are going on right now in your body as you read this sentence. As your eyes read the page, an image is transmitted to your brain to be decoded. Once the message is received, you further process it to become meaningful. All the while, your breathing continues and your blood, containing life-sustaining oxygen, is pumped to the organs of your body which need it to continue to function. You are a miracle as you sit and read this book, and there are billions of beings just like you. We all inhabit a planet hurtling through space at just the right speed and perfect distance from a sun that is burning at the precise temperature to promote life.

Yet some would tell us that all this is just an accident.

Look at the sentence above for just a moment and then answer my first question of this chapter. How did you get here? Would you please answer that question with all the integrity you can conjure up? If your explanation includes a Creator, then wouldn't it be logical to want to seek and know the Being who created you? As created beings, our lives would only make sense within a relationship with the One who made us. To seek Him would be the most natural activity with which one could become engaged.

Not long ago, our family visited Philadelphia and saw the house where Thomas Jefferson penned the Declaration of Independence. We viewed one of the earliest copies signed by the men who adopted it (the original resides in Washington at the National Archives). There was a family standing beside us admiring one of the signatures, which was that of one of their ancestors. They had great pride as they looked at the handwriting of someone related to them. They, in some way, felt that they had participated in the history of this important document and had tracked down the document in Philadelphia. It gave them a sense of their family's history.

People spend a lot of time and money to research their family of origin. They may travel to far parts of our country and the world just to find out who their great-great-grandfather was and what he did in this world. They are proud when they discover he fought at Gettysburg, or signed the Declaration of Independence.

Why don't we want to spend time tracking down our Creator? Every day we see His signature across the skies and in the people with whom we come in contact. If God is our Creator and if we are really made in His image (Genesis 1:27) then shouldn't we want to find out more about Him and how He feels about us? It would only seem logical. Since we are people who thrive on sound ideas, one would think each of us would be on a journey to meet and know this God who designed us.

When people see my sons Ryan and Chris, they say that

they look like me. Both my sons like to tell jokes, just like me. My friends tell me that they carry themselves like me. People say, "It's amazing; it is just like looking at you." In the same way, when people see believers, they can see, in a small way, what God is like. As God's creations, we are made in His image. We do not perfectly resemble Him, because of the sin in our lives, but God can still be seen through the imperfect actions and emotions of those who follow Him.

If we are created to be like God, then our hearts are only truly happy when we are with Him. Evangelists have reminded us that "there is a God-shaped vacuum in everyone of us." St. Augustine said, "Our souls are restless until we find our rest in Him." This attraction is as natural as the baby who hears her parents' voices at birth and is drawn to them. Many men I know are haunted into their old age by a broken relationship with their father. We are unsatisfied in our lives until we properly know our parents. I have known men and women who are adopted and wanted desperately to connect with their birth parents. They want to know those who brought them physically into this world. We want to know and love those who have begotten us.

An early theologian compared this to the phenomenon of a baby bird that seeks its mother. He cited the illustration that sometimes partridges will steal the eggs of other birds and hatch them. Yet upon their hatching, if the baby bird hears the cry of its natural mother, it will desert the partridge and seek its true parent. Once again, we turn to Richard Foster and Gayle Beebe for further enlightenment:

Each one of us has a longing to know—to know right from wrong, to know the ultimate destiny of our life, to know how we can make a meaningful contribution with our gifts and abilities. We want to know where we were born, how we were raised and what we will do in the future. We want to know that we are part of something greater than ourselves. Ultimately, we want to know that we belong to God.[1] This knowledge never comes quickly or completely; it must develop over time as we deepen in understanding our life with God.[2]

We live in a world that has "stolen" us away from our real Father. Wrapped in an envelope of chaos and circumstance, we are distracted from Him who can give us our true life. From time to time, we hear His call and we hearken back to the One who created us. Yet, unlike the birds, we are torn with a desire to be acceptable and successful in a world that will not be our permanent home. While our need to know our Father is great, so are the distractions of this world, which can serve as a barrier to our knowledge of Him who gave us life. The fact remains that we were made to know and love Him who made us for a purpose in His kingdom.

This heart to understand God begins as a yearning to know our Creator. It moves us to praise the One who is much more powerful than we can imagine.

---

[1] Author's note: Foster and Beebe here are describing the *Christian's* pursuit of God. The one who has not received God's forgiveness through Christ, does not want to know that he belongs to God.

[2] Foster and Beebe, p. 87.

David said in the Psalms:

> For you created my inmost being;
>> you knit me together in my mother's womb.

> I praise you because I am fearfully and wonder-
> fully made;
>> your works are wonderful,
>> I know that full well.

> My frame was not hidden from you
>> when I was made in the secret place.
>> When I was woven together in the depths of the earth,
>> your eyes saw my unformed body.

> All the days ordained for me were written in
> your book
>> before one of them came to be.

—PSALM 139:13–16

Paul says in Colossians:

> For by him all things were created: things in heaven and
> on earth, visible and invisible, whether thrones or pow-
> ers or rulers or authorities; all things were created by him
> and for him.

—COLOSSIANS 1:16

As Christians come to understand, without a doubt, that God is the Creator, their faith will be strengthened. It is of great importance to our growth that we understand why we believe in the Creator God. We must work through our opinions of the validity of Creation and the illogic of Darwinism, random big bang theories, and all the other explanations of our existence. To examine the theories in light of Scripture is not just a good idea; it is vital. Some non-believers do not do it because they are afraid of what they might find. If they discover a true God, they will have to admit that they are morally accountable to Him. Most, if not all, non-believers do not want to be morally accountable to anyone or anything! If they can cast any uncertainty in their own minds toward the reality of a Creator, they think they are "free" from any claim that He might have on their lives and behavior. The awful truth for committed non-believers is that if God is the Creator, they are creatures made like God and have a need to come into relationship with Him. Their life is no longer their own, but has a part in the kingdom of the Creator. This ownership carries with it responsibilities that they do not want.

Maybe this is what Paul was thinking when he said to the Philippians, ". . . continue to work out your salvation with fear and trembling" (Philippians 2:12). We must seek to understand what it means that God created us. What are the implications for our lives? Who are we supposed to be? What are we destined to do? No wonder Paul called it "work." It may seem daunting, yet we cannot think of God in any other way than the fact that He is our Creator. If He is not Creator, then how can He be God? John Murray, former professor at Princeton and Westminster seminaries, put it this way:

> So far then as we are concerned, we can never think of God without thinking of God as God and of ourselves as his creatures. In other words, the thought of creation, the thought of our dependence upon God, is implicated

in any true thought we entertain with respect to God. Without the concept of creation, then, we cannot think even one right thought of God. Hence the significance of creation for our conception of God and therefore the Christian position.[3]

Once we ascertain the truth, that a great God created our world, our lives will be changed. We will find once we are acquainted with the God of life, we will fall in love with Him. David, finishing his thoughts of his Creator in Psalm 139:17 says, "How precious to me are your thoughts, O God! How vast is the sum of them!" He was blown away by his love for God. David wanted to know what God was thinking. He needed to be near Him and have a right relationship with Him. We should want nothing less than that.

As great as the fact that He created the world is the truth that He created you and me. He crafted us with the skill of the highest artisan as well as with the care and love of a Father. He stood back after His creation of man and woman and stated that His work was very good (Genesis 1:31). They were planned with a purpose in mind. Their lives had meaning because God willed it so. He made you and me for a reason, too. Scripture says, "For we are God's workmanship, created in Christ Jesus to do good works, which God prepared in advance for us to do" (Ephesians 2:10).

The gospel story revolves around God's creation of man and man's subsequent rebellion. God made man in His

---

[3] John Murray, *Collected Writings of John Murray, Vol. I: The Claims of Truth* (The Banner of Truth, Carlisle, Pennsylvania, 1976), p. 326.

own image (Genesis 1:27). At that point, God was pleased with man and the two had a perfect relationship. Man was sinless and able to obey God perfectly. The fall of man occurred when the man (and the woman) decided to *not* obey God and go their own way (Genesis 3). As a result of their sin, Adam and Eve were cast out of the Garden and from their relationship with God. They were no longer able to obey Him perfectly. God was no longer pleased with the man and woman, yet He did not abandon His creation. (It is here that I make the distinction between God being pleased with His creation and God being displeased with man as part of that creation. God cannot be pleased with the sin of man, but can be pleased with His creation of man.)

Without God, man would be doomed to live outside of the Kingdom for which he was created. God, in His infinite love, came to earth as Jesus Christ in order to save His creation. Jesus lived a sinless life on earth as a man and therefore, remained in perfect relationship with God in Heaven. His sinless life was sacrificed on the cross as God's payment for our sins. We were returned or reconciled, as Colossians 1:22 states. For those of us who have trusted Christ for our salvation, God looks at us through the sacrifice of Jesus and forgives our rebellion against Him. Here's a passage that most of us are familiar with, "For God so loved the world that He gave his one and only Son, that whoever believes in Him shall not perish but have eternal life" (John 3:16). God loved us so much that He personally came to earth in order to rescue us from our sin. Here is love that can only exist in the One who is love Himself. Look at how John expressed it:

Dear friends, let us love one another, for love comes
from God. Everyone who loves has been born of God and
knows God. Whoever does not love does not know God,
because God is love. This is how God showed His love
among us: He sent His one and only Son into the world
that we might live through Him. This is love: not that we
loved God, but that He loved us and sent His Son as an
atoning sacrifice for our sins. Dear friends, since God so
loved us, we also ought to love one another.

—1 JOHN 4:7–11

I once heard a story of a young child called to present a
speech in front of his entire school. The boy had suffered for
years with several deformities, the most obvious one being
a hunchback-like defect on his shoulder. The occasion of
standing up in front of a large group of people was frightening to him. As he gave his speech, another boy loudly whis-
pered, "Hey kid, get that pack off your back." The speaker
began to stammer and then stopped altogether. After a
moment of uncomfortable silence, a man in the audience
walked up front and stood with the humiliated student. He
carefully worded his reply. "You know I just want everyone
to know what I think of this boy. I am so proud of him and
of the work that he has put into his speech. I happen to
know that he stayed up two nights in a row in order to do
the research for this talk. He has done everything that he
could do so his presentation would be just right for you.
And I'm really proud of him for that. But most of all, I am
proud of him just because . . . he is my son." And with the
pride that only a father could exhibit, he led his son off the

stage. Despite the tears, a smile was seen on the face of the boy as he walked with his father, the one man on earth who could have redeemed the situation.

God views you in that manner because He designed you and gave the ultimate sacrifice so that you might become new. With the love only a Father can give, He built into you the talents and gifts you would need to live the life He has planned for you. He redeemed you through the life of Jesus Christ. No one knows and loves you like the Great Creator of Life. There is no other place on earth where you can experience love and worth as you can as you come to know the God who made you. Our God came to stand with you in the Man, Jesus Christ. He has come to replace your distress with hope through a relationship with the One who knows us intimately.

Who would throw away a piece of art that was skillfully designed and delicately made? God individually designed you. How could you discard your relationship with this Creator who has great purpose for you within His world? God intended that His work in you would become a part of His kingdom. He prepared opportunities for you from the very beginning that would be significant, that would thrill your heart. Not only would your works be meaningful to you but they would also make Him smile and laugh and cry as He saw you fulfill the purpose that He gave you from the beginning.

We love God because He created us and He did so with a love that we can never fathom. In the next chapter, we will take a closer look at that.

Discussion Questions

1. Do you ever have trouble believing that God created the world? What causes you to think that He did or didn't?

2. What is the most compelling reason to believe in the Creation story?

3. If God is in fact your Creator, with what implications are you left?

4. What causes you to be reminded that you are made in God's image?

5. Why is it hard to believe that we are God's craftsmanship?

Chapter Three

Because He First Loved Us

How great is the love the Father has lavished on us, that we should be called children of God! And that is what we are! The reason the world does not know us is that it did not know him. Dear friends, now we are children of God, and what we will be has not yet been made known. But we know that when he appears, we shall be like him, for we shall see him as he is. Everyone who has this hope in him purifies himself, just as he is pure.

1 JOHN 3:1–3

WHEN I WAS a kid growing up in Tyler, Texas, we went to church. I mean we *really* went to church. At the age of five, I had a drug problem: I was constantly drug back and forth to church! The doors didn't open without the Wernettes. We were there on Sunday morning, Sunday night, and Wednesday prayer meeting. One of my Sunday school friends even asked me if my dad owned the church. Now, of course, he did not own the church, but he *did* serve on the deacon board, count the money in the offering plate, announce new members when they joined, usher folks to their seats, and who knows what else. I would help him count the money after the service on Sunday morning and then ride with him to take the money downtown to the bank. To say we were heavily involved in the church would be an understatement.

Of course, I was a regular at Sunday school. I knew all the songs. I could belt them out when the situation called for it. One song we sang a lot was, "Oh, How I Love Jesus." I never truly understood why Jesus loved me. I just knew that the song said that because of His love, I loved Him. Here it is. Sing along if you want to:

> There is a Name I love to hear,
> I love to sing its worth;
> It sounds like music in my ear,
> The sweetest Name on earth.
>
> Oh, how I love Jesus,
> Oh, how I love Jesus,
> Oh, how I love Jesus,
> Because He first loved me!
>
> It tells me of a Savior's love,
> Who died to set me free;
> It tells me of His precious blood,
> The sinner's perfect plea.
>
> Oh, how I love Jesus,
> Oh, how I love Jesus,
> Oh, how I love Jesus,
> Because He first loved me!
>
> It tells of One whose loving heart
> Can feel my deepest woe;
> Who in each sorrow bears a part
> That none can bear below.

Oh, how I love Jesus,
Oh, how I love Jesus,
Oh, how I love Jesus,
Because He first loved me![1]

As I grew up, I began to learn what the Scriptures said, and I learned that the lyrics mirrored the Bible. Jesus really did love me. That love did draw me to love Him. First John 4:19 tells me that I love because He first loved me. The reason I am able to love God is because He first loved me. He shows me what love is through His love for me.

How do I know God loves me? He came to earth to visit me (and you). Here is what John said: "This is how God showed his love among us: He sent his one and only Son into the world that we might live through him" (1 John 4:9). In John 1:14 we are told, "The Word became flesh and made his dwelling among us. We have seen his glory, the glory of the One and Only who came from the Father, full of grace and truth." "Made his dwelling" in the original Greek language meant "tabernacled." It means God came to earth and pitched His tent with us.

What a concept! God came and camped out with us. Have you ever travelled with someone outside your immediate family? You learn about them very quickly. You come to know when they like to eat and what kind of food they prefer. During your time with them, you will come to know when they like to get up and how many activities they like

---

[1]   Frederick Whitfield, "Oh, How I Love Jesus," 1855.

to do during the day. But, if you go *camping* with them, you get an entirely different look. Now you are eye to eye with them for twenty-four hours a day. Do not go backpacking or camping with someone unless you are sure you really like that person. And even then, you may wind up in conflict. You are just too close, and their habits affect you in ways that you cannot imagine.

Amazingly, God came to earth and walked in our shoes. He lived as a man. He didn't do it out of duty. He did it because He was crazy about His creations. God couldn't stay away from us! He wanted us to know Him so much He came to live with us—to pitch His tent with us. God camped out on earth with us so we could see Him in a whole new way. The man Jesus was God on earth. He entered our world because we are so dear to Him. His presence on this earth is a testimony that He loves us greatly.

My dad makes a four-hour drive to Houston from Tyler every so often just to come see my family and me. Before she passed away, my mom would come also. Dad has come to see Little League baseball games, to spend Christmas with us, or just for a visit. He has never mentioned that it was his duty to come to Houston. He does it because he wants to be with us. I never get over the idea that he drives a long way and alters his schedule just so he can come and see how we are doing.

Listen to this: God made time in His schedule to come to see us. At just the right time in history, He took on the form of a man named Jesus and came to earth. He did not just send a note or a bouquet; He actually came down to earth and lived on the same planet as we do. He worked like we do. He got hungry like we do. He had friends that He hung out with, just like we do. He was a real man who was tempted just like we are, except He never sinned (Hebrews 4:15). As a human being, Jesus set a perfect model for us. He demonstrated how to truly live as a man. He not only showed us what God is like, He showed us what man could be like. God took the time to model perfect obedience through His Son.

My dad taught me to play baseball. He would stop what he was doing and go outside and play pitch. He threw to me on countless occasions so that I could learn to hit. When I was little, he would get down on his knees—on my level— to teach me how to catch and throw. When I was older, he coached my teams. He allowed his life to be interrupted by me. That's what God did, except in a much greater way. He determined that His life would be spent with His people. *God got down on our level.*

Chapter 5 of Luke's gospel displays how God came to "hang out" with people. In this passage, Jesus was teaching, and as He finished, He noticed two boats by the water. One of the fishermen was Simon, who would later be known as Peter. Jesus told him to go back and throw the nets out for a big catch. Remember, these guys were professional fishermen. They knew how to fish. Maybe they looked at each other and rolled their eyes. But there was something about Jesus that told them just to do it. Simon told Jesus even though they had fished all night, they would do what He said. We know how this story goes. They caught fish. I mean a lot of fish. Their nets began to break. They signaled for another boat to come over to them, and when they brought the catch aboard, the boats started sinking. Simon Peter's reaction is recorded in verse 8: "When Simon Peter saw this, he fell at Jesus' knees and said, 'Go away from me, Lord; I am a sinful man!'" Peter recognized that it was God who was visiting him. He knew that he was not worthy to stand beside this holy God who had appeared before him in the form of this man, Jesus.

Jesus continued His journey "among us" as next He healed a leper. He reached out and touched the man (v. 13). Can you imagine God touching the sores of a leper? Then He encountered the paralytic man carried to a house by his friends. So many people wanted to see Jesus that the house was full. No problem. They just went upstairs and tore the roof off and let him down with ropes. Jesus healed the man's body but first forgave his sin. The teachers of the law who were present thought, "Who is this fellow who speaks blasphemy? Who can forgive sins but God alone?" Right. It *is* only God who can erase our sins. It was God standing there with them, reading their minds and healing the man who needed help.

Toward the end of Luke 5, there is still another occurrence where Jesus stepped down to be with His people. Jesus met the tax collector, Levi. When Jesus directed him to follow, Levi got up, left EVERYTHING and followed Jesus. "Everything" would have no doubt been a handsome amount of money since the tax business was a lucrative one in which to be involved. Levi was so excited about his new friend that he threw a big party at his house. Who did he invite to meet Jesus? Why, his friends, of course. There were tax collectors and a host of "sinners." There is no telling who these people were and what they had done. The teachers of the law asked Jesus' disciples, "Why do you eat and drink with tax collectors and 'sinners'?" The disciples did not know to tell them: *Uh, this is God and He has come down from Heaven to "hang out" for a while.* Instead, Jesus Himself answered them, "It is not the healthy who need a doctor, but the sick. I have not come to call the righteous, but sinners to repentance." It was these kinds of people who needed Him. They were the ones who knew that they were ill. They were sick and condemned in their sins.

What was going on? God had come to earth and loved these people in ways they could understand. He was touching their needs and in most cases, touching *them* physically. God was demonstrating His great love for them and approaching people who did not know who He was. He loved them before they loved Him. He was, as Frederick Whitfield wrote in "Oh, How I Love Jesus," "One whose loving heart can feel my deepest woe / Who in each sorrow bears a part that none can bear below." It was God who had interrupted His day in order to love these people. How could they not love Him back?

God acts in such a way that it clearly communicates His love. He can do nothing less since He is made of love. John says in 1 John 4:8, "Whoever does not love does not know God, because God is love." The essence of God is love. It is a pure love that has no motive or agenda. He loves us because

He wants to, not because of what we have done. In fact, He loves us *despite* what we do. Knowing that His creatures would reject him, God came to earth. And that is how we know He loves us. Look at how Paul described this love:

> You see, at just the right time, when we were still power-less, Christ died for the ungodly. Very rarely will anyone die for a righteous man, though for a good man some-one might possibly dare to die. But God demonstrates his own love for us in this: While we were still sinners, Christ died for us.
>
> —ROMANS 5:6–8

While we were still sinners, Christ died for us. He came to earth and died for us, not *because* we were His best friends. He did it *despite* the fact that we were sinners who openly rebelled against Him. While my dad might come to visit me, he would probably *not* go out of his way to see his worst enemy. Who of you would take two weeks of vacation and go visit someone who hates you? No one. But that is what God did, except that He stayed for thirty-three years! He came to earth knowing that we would reject Him and that we would obey everyone else in the world, except Him. We are true enemies of God as we sin and draw others in with us. God just keeps on loving us and allows us to enjoy the world that He made. He loved us *way* before we loved Him.

How could we not want to learn more about a God who loves us when we are most unlovable? As humans, we want to get away from those who can't behave. We shy away from people who brag or curse or have to be the center of attention. If someone hates us, our natural reaction is to hate that person right back. When we despised God and were His enemies He looked at us as a Father and came to earth to retrieve us. He wants His creations to know His love and live with the purpose He placed in them.

Now I see what the song, "Oh, How I Love Jesus," meant. I love Jesus because He first loved me. I cannot truly experience the life of Jesus and turn away unaffected. His life among us stirs my thinking that maybe there is purpose in this chaos. There must be a great mission for me, as well as for others who have followed Him. The truths of the life of Jesus compel me (2 Corinthians 5:14) to seek Him and His kingdom.

The Scripture that began this chapter (1 John 3:1–3) says that God showed His love for us by calling us as His children. Some of you have been adopted, and you know what it feels like to be known as someone's child. At one time you had no parents, but "strangers" were willing to give you their name, call you their child, and have accepted you. What an honor that is. I have jokingly asked some of my rich friends if they would adopt me. I would like to take advantage of their wealth when I really do not deserve it. What if the Creator of the Universe wants to adopt you? You do not deserve it, but wouldn't it be great to be in the family of the One who thought up the world? It *is* possible. He loves you and has proven His love in a unique way.

This brings up one more reason why we should love God. And it is the most compelling reason of all. The best part of the story follows in the next chapter.

Discussion Questions

1. Have you ever been camping or on vacation with a group of people that you didn't know very well? What did you learn about them?

2. If you were God, would you have come down and "camped out" on earth? Why or why not? How would you have chosen to express your love to the world?

3. Who in your life has loved you more than you deserved? Why did they do it?

4. Who do you know who has left something that they loved in order to follow Jesus? What did they do?

5. If you believe God loved us when we were His enemies, how does that affect your concept of God?

Chapter Four

Because He Gave His Life For Us

This is how God showed his love among us: He sent
his one and only Son into the world that we might live
through him. This is love: not that we loved God, but
that he loved us and sent his Son as an atoning sacrifice
for our sins.

—1 JOHN 4:9–10

IN HIS BOOK *The Importance of Being Foolish*, Brennan
Manning tells the following story. Two United States Marine
Corps corporals were behind enemy lines during some of
the heaviest fighting of the Korean War. The two men were
Tim Casey and Jack Robison.[1] As often happens to comrades
in arms, the two soldiers had become great friends during
the year they had served together.

A little after midnight, with a light snow falling, a hand
grenade was lobbed into their bunker by the enemy. The
grenade landed right between the two men. Without hes-
itation and without saying a word, Tim Casey flicked his
cigarette butt aside and threw himself on the grenade,

---

[1] I have repeated the story here using the names Manning does in
his book, however it should be noted that many believe the story is
actually about Manning himself.

absorbing the blow. As Manning explains it, he winked at his friend Jack . . . and rolled over dead.

After the war, Jack Robison changed his first name to Casey to honor his friend's sacrifice. He also became a friend of Tim's mother and visited her regularly at her home in Chicago. On one of those visits, Casey Robison—now a Catholic priest—was feeling gloomy and depressed.

> After dinner they sat in the living room having a drink and reminiscing about the days when Tim was alive. The priest's depression lingered. Unexpectedly he asked, "Ma, do you think [Tim] really loved me?"
>
> She laughed. "Oh, Jack, ya sure got a way with ya." It was a faint Irish brogue. "Ya can't ever be serious."
>
> "I am serious," Robison replied.
>
> There was fear in her eyes. "Now stop funnin' me, Jack."
>
> "I'm not funnin, Ma."
>
> She looked at him in disbelief. Then fear turned to fury . . . she stood up and screamed, ". . . man, what more could he ha' done fer ya?"
>
> Then she sank back in the chair, buried her head in her bosom, and began to sob. Over and over again the same phrase was endlessly, unbearably repeated: "What more could he ha' done fer ya?"[2]

What more could God do for us? The Bible tells us that one day Jesus, God on earth, went to a cross and died in order that we would be forgiven. Yes, in His great power

---

[2] Brennan Manning, *The Importance of Being Foolish* (Harper, San Francisco, California, 2005), pp. 63–64.

and sovereignty He could have just declared us forgiven. He has the power and authority to do so. But in His divine wisdom, He gave us more than a declaration of innocence. God showed us both His love and justice. The death of Jesus satisfied the law. In any culture, a guilty party must suffer the penalty for his sin. Jesus bore the penalty of our sin. He suffered the death that rightly belonged to us. First Peter 2:24 says, "He himself bore our sins in his body on the tree, so that we might die to sins and live for righteousness; by his wounds you have been healed."

We are told that a picture is worth a thousand words. If this is true, how many words is a life event worth? The death of Jesus displayed once for all that men and women who take His name and follow Him will be forgiven and invited into the kingdom of God. In the death of Jesus, God was reconciling all things—including us—back to Himself (Colossians 1:20). He was dying the death that our sin called for us to die and giving us a moment in history that we could view for ages to come.

I would highly recommend that before proceeding to read further that you locate a Bible and read one or more of the accounts of Jesus' arrest, trial, and crucifixion (Matthew 26–27, Mark 14–15, Luke 22–23, John 13, 18–19). Since these reports form the foundation of our faith, we should be very familiar with the historical record that they provide. Why do we wait until one or two days at Easter to read the stories of Jesus' great work? These accounts should be read on a regular basis to ensure our knowledge of these Gospel descriptions.

In his great work, *The Cross of Christ*, John Stott focuses on three moments of Jesus' ordeal on the most important day of history.[3] He first takes a look at the event that we call the Last Supper. Scripture says:

> And he took bread, gave thanks and broke it, and gave it to them, saying, "This is my body given for you; do this in remembrance of me." In the same way, after the supper he took the cup, saying, "This cup is the new covenant in my blood, which is poured out for you."
>
> —LUKE 22:19–21

Jesus administers the Passover supper, but adds new meaning to it. Jesus distributed the bread, which He now gave as His Body that He was giving for them. The wine no longer symbolized the blood of a lamb; it would now represent the Blood of *the* Lamb, which was to be shed for the forgiveness of sin. Both of the elements were given to each of the disciples with the expectation that they would individually eat and drink them in remembrance of Jesus.

The Last Supper represents the centrality of the cross, the purpose of the cross, and the personal need to appropriate the death of Christ. The sacrament has come to be celebrated, not just once, but regularly, in remembrance of Jesus. He told His disciples to "do this in remembrance of me." First, the cross is the cornerstone of our Christian lives. The elements of our communion remind us of Jesus' death

---

[3] John Stott, *The Cross of Christ* (InterVarsity Press, Downers Grove, Illinois, 1986), pp. 66–84.

and of God's great forgiveness of us. Without the cross there is no Christian life. It stands at the center of our relationship with our Creator. Second, the elements also serve to remind us that Jesus died in order that we might have a living relationship with God. As He served the wine, Jesus said, "This is my blood of the covenant, which is poured out for many for the forgiveness of sins" (Matthew 26:28). We are allowed to come to God only because He enables us to do so through the blood of Christ, which serves as forgiveness of our sins. We have no right or ability save for that empowerment. There is nothing we can do to put ourselves right with God, except to trust in the great sacrifice of Jesus. We can perform no good deed to erase the sin that will eternally separate us from God. Only the final sacrifice of Christ on the cross can make us acceptable to God. Finally, the elements had to be individually consumed by each disciple. One cannot accept the gift of forgiveness for anyone else any more than one can eat a meal for someone else. We each have a need to come to Jesus alone. Many have leaned on the faith of their parents, assuming that a relationship with God can be passed on generationally. While it is a great advantage, the faith of one's father or mother does not guarantee the child will possess a saving knowledge of Christ. Faith is a personal decision.

In the second scene on which Stott focuses, we see Jesus in the Garden of Gethsemane. He led His disciples out of town and to a retreat place at which they frequently assembled. Mark describes the events in Mark 14:32–42. If anyone believes that the cross was not difficult for Jesus, one must only look at this passage to discover otherwise. As He began to be "deeply distressed and troubled," Jesus told His disciples, "My soul is overwhelmed with sorrow to the point of death." Jesus knew what the next few hours would bring, and He desperately wanted companionship and comfort. He took His three closest friends (Peter, James, and John) aside and began to pray. Jesus asked God to "take this cup from me, yet not my will, but yours be done." (Luke 22:42) As He prayed, He was so troubled that the Bible said His sweat was "like drops of blood falling to the ground." (Luke 22:44) How did His disciples comfort Him during this terrible time? They went to sleep. His best friends and most trusted companions "deserted" Him to their own sleep when He needed them most. How much did Jesus love us? He sat alone in His own terror and trusted His future to His heavenly Father. He did this without even so much as one earthly friend who would sit up with Him during the struggle.

The third and last scene that Stott looks at is Jesus on the cross and His cry to God, the Father. In His last moments of agony, He cried out, "My God, my God, why have you forsaken me?" (Mark 15:34). It was at this moment, that the sins of the world were laid upon Jesus, and He was separated from God, the Father. He referred to God, not as His Father, but as "my God." At that instant, He was alone with the guilt and embarrassment of our sin. His Father would not look upon the guilty form on the cross, and Jesus felt an isolation that has never been equaled on earth. He cried, "My God, why have you forsaken me?" so we would not have to say it ourselves. The forgiveness that was extended to us that day would insure that we would never have to be separated from God by our personal rebellion. Our sin leads to a sure death. Jesus experienced in full the death that is rightfully ours. How much does God love us? He gave the life of Himself, in Jesus Christ, on the cross. Did He do it knowing that we were great people and that we would embrace this sacrifice with arms wide open? Hardly. Paul described it in his letter to the Ephesians like this:

> All of us also lived among them at one time, gratifying the cravings of our sinful nature and following its desires and thoughts. Like the rest, we were by nature objects of wrath. But because of his great love for us, God, who is rich in mercy, made us alive with Christ even when we were dead in transgressions—it is by grace you have been saved.
>
> —EPHESIANS 2:3–5

We, by our nature, are objects of wrath. We hate to hear this! But this opens up a wonderful look at the love of God. At a time that we were more interested in earthly riches and power, God came to earth and laid His life down for us. Knowing that many would reject His action, God went to the cross. God knew full well that men would invent other ways to "be saved." Even though men would concoct religions in which they attempt to find other pathways to God, He still showed mankind His love on the cross. Man is dead without the sacrifice of Christ. He has no chance. Yet, in Christ's great love, He takes our sinful condition and converts it to one of life. We are made alive in Christ! Jesus suffered an ex-cruciating death to return each one of us, once and for all, to our Creator. This grace (undeserved favor) was extended to us through the death of Jesus on the cross.

How could one look at the crucifixion and not be changed forever? Here we see love like we have never seen before or will ever experience on this earth again. Scripture says, "For God so loved the world that he gave his one and only Son, that whoever believes in him shall not perish but have eternal life" (John 3:16). John also said it like this, "This is how God showed his love among us: He sent his one and only Son into the world that we might live through him. This is love: not that we loved God, but that he loved us and sent his Son as an atoning sacrifice for our sins" (1 John 4:9–10).

Just as Jack Robison took his friend's name, so we take up the name of Christ as we come to know His great love for us. We become Christians (literally meaning *Christ ones*). His sacrifice changes our lives. It reroutes our lives to be something that we would never have imagined. It includes us to be a part of God's world. We, as humans who are full of sin, are freed to participate with God in His plans for the world as if we were perfect, just like Jesus. God sees us as forgiven through the death of Christ, and we no longer must dwell in the guilt and embarrassment of our many shortcomings.

Many turn away from God and say that He is vindictive because He promises to punish those who refuse His offer of forgiveness. Some say that if God were real He would show His love to the world in a more generous way. How could there be a better way to display love than in the giving of One's life? Where in this world is there love like that? The answer is nowhere! The cross of Christ clearly tells us that God loves us.

Jesus offers us a path by which we might journey with Him straight to the heart of God. If this is the journey that Jesus offers us to take with Him, the cross marks the trailhead. It is beginning of the trail. When we become lost within the world that seeks to move us to other paths, the cross is our landmark by which we can find our way back to the truth of God's love.

Dr. John Bisagno, retired senior pastor of Houston's First Baptist Church, once concluded a sermon with a story that illustrates the centrality of the cross to our faith. There was a young boy who wandered away from his home and became lost, not far from his neighborhood. Seeing a policeman, the child waved him over. The officer asked the boy if he knew his address and the boy said that he did not. When asked if he could remember what his house looked like or what cars might be in the driveway, the youngster again said that he did not know. All at once the boy remembered something. "Wait, mister," he said. "I do remember something. There is a large church right behind my house. That church has a large steeple on it, and on the top of the steeple is a cross. If I could just see that cross, I think that I could recognize my neighborhood." Now the boy beamed and said, "Just hold me up, mister, and show me that cross, and I know that I will find my way home from there."

We need to hold each other up so that we might see the cross. It will lead us right back to God's love. It will help us find our way home to the love of God. The message of the cross is one of God's acceptance of us. God's love is seen clearly in His great sacrifice. It will draw us back to Him when all else leads us away.

Maybe you have been reading this so far and now realize that you are not following Jesus in your life. If you find that you really don't know Jesus, stop and listen.

Ask Jesus to forgive you of your sins in order that you might know His love. In His forgiveness, He will give you what you have always wanted—real acceptance and love. Becoming a follower of Jesus starts with a small first step. It begins by accepting the gift of forgiveness offered by your Creator in the life of Jesus. It is first a matter of acknowledging who Jesus is. He is God come to earth (read Colossians 1:15–23). Jesus created all things and contains the fullness of God. God came to earth as Jesus Christ in order to reconcile (bring back) to Himself all things. That includes you as well as everything contained in the universe. We have become estranged (alienated) from God (Colossians 1:21), but He stepped out of eternity in order to return His people to a proper relationship with Him.

Secondly, in order to become a follower of Christ, we ask His permission to do so. We admit that we have turned away and followed other gods. Scripture tells us that all of us have rebelled against God (Romans 3:10–18 and 23). Through Jesus' death on the cross, God offers forgiveness to those who ask Him for it (Romans 3:24–26). The Bible tells us in Romans 10:9–13, that in order to be saved (returned to God), one must confess that Jesus is the Lord of his life. In that, one is declaring that he will love and obey his new Lord. The passage in Romans 10 also says that one must believe that God raised Him from the dead. One must acknowledge the identity of Jesus and recognize that He has command over life and death.

Romans 10:13 says that all who call on the name of the Lord will be saved. That is God's guarantee. If you turn to Him, He will not ignore you. He will not forget you. It is a lifetime commitment by God to you! Yes, there is much in life that will follow and yes, there will be difficult times. You will be asked to give up your priorities for the sake of the kingdom of God. You may be required to follow Christ into scary places. But remember: When you trust God with your life, your dreams, and your possessions, you will find the love that you have always wanted. There is nothing on this earth that is better than the love of God. If this matter is not settled in your life, take care of it today. Eternity is too good to waste!

Discussion Questions

1 How does the story Brennan Manning tells of Jack Robison influence you? What does it teach you about sacrifice? What does it teach you about carrying someone else's name?

2. What would you have thought if you had personally

observed the events of the Last Supper? What
questions would you like to ask about Jesus' remarks
to Judas (Matthew 26:25, Mark 14:18, John 13:26–30)?

3. Why did the disciples fall asleep in the garden while
Jesus prayed? What would you think about your
friends if they slept while you were in an hour of
need?

4. Why should we be cautious and not casual about
calling ourselves "Christians"?

5. How does the cross point a Christian to the way
"home," as in the story that concludes this chapter?

Chapter Five

"God, Help Me Love You More"

When they had finished eating, Jesus said to Simon Peter, "Simon son of John, do you truly love me more than these?"

"Yes, Lord," he said, "you know that I love you."

Jesus said, "Feed my lambs."

Again Jesus said, "Simon son of John, do you truly love me?"

He answered, "Yes, Lord, you know that I love you."

Jesus said, "Take care of my sheep."

The third time he said to him, "Simon son of John, do you love me?"

Peter was hurt because Jesus asked him the third time, "Do you love me?" He said, "Lord, you know all things; you know that I love you."

Jesus said, "Feed my sheep. I tell you the truth, when you were younger you dressed yourself and went where you wanted; but when you are old you will stretch out your hands, and someone else will dress you and lead you where you do not want to go." Jesus said this to indicate the kind of death by which Peter would glorify God. Then he said to him, "Follow me!"

—JOHN 21:15–19

LOVE GOD WITH all my heart, soul, mind, and strength? Are you kidding me? I'm having enough trouble learning to love my wife and kids. And they live right here with me. If we know ourselves, as well as Scripture, we will realize the difficulty of loving God. We are so full of ourselves that the task seems impossible. How can people like you and me ever be able to love God? Jesus commanded us to love God first and then others and finally ourselves. We do just the opposite. How will we ever change that?

Scripture clearly teaches that we are hopelessly lost in our sin without Christ. Romans 3:10–18 states:

> As it is written: "There is no one righteous, not even one; there is no one who understands, no one who seeks God. All have turned away, they have together become worthless; there is no one who does good, not even one." "Their throats are open graves; their tongues practice deceit." "The poison of vipers is on their lips." "Their mouths are full of cursing and bitterness." "Their feet are swift to shed blood; ruin and misery mark their ways, and the way of peace they do not know." "There is no fear of God before their eyes."

Yet when Christ takes over a life, doesn't all this change? As a Christian, are we not able to withstand the sin that drives us away from God? If we listen to Paul in his discussion in Romans 7, we still live in the shadow of our sin. We cannot do what we want to do but wind up doing what we do not want to do. We want to love God, but somehow we love other things. There is a constant battle within each of us. We know that loving God is the greater good, yet we slide back into loving temporary things.

Peter was Jesus' great earthly project. Jesus spent countless days and nights with all the disciples, yet He seemed to pay special attention to Peter. He took Peter with Him as He performed miracles. He sent him on mission trips and then debriefed him when he returned. He invited Peter, James, and John to a really neat mountain retreat where they saw Him transfigured (Mark 9:2). Peter even walked on water just like Jesus did. If anyone ever loved Jesus, it would have been Peter.

We know what happened when the heat was turned up. When Peter followed Jesus after He was arrested (something that I probably would not have done), he got so scared that a little girl—a little servant girl!—caused him to deny that he had ever known Jesus (Mark 14:66–72). Here was a big, strong fisherman who was not afraid of anything, but he became frightened and let this girl's verbal challenge run him off. How could Jesus ever forgive him? At the point where Jesus needed a friend more than ever, Peter loved himself and his own safety so much that he said that he did not know Jesus—and he even cursed as he said it.

What would Jesus say about that? It took Peter several days to find out. In Mark 16, the women discovered that Jesus was no longer in the grave. In the tomb was a young man, dressed in white, presumably an angel. He told them to, ". . . go, tell his disciples and Peter" that He would meet them in Galilee. Can you imagine the reaction when the women told the disciples? As they told their story, maybe they looked at Peter and said, "Peter, he specifically told us to tell *you* to meet Jesus in Galilee." The angel had singled out Peter, the one who now appeared to be least qualified to love Jesus. He was so afraid, so selfish, so self-centered. But the angel specifically mentioned him and told him to go find Jesus. Since angels are messengers from God, we must assume that God was reaching out to Peter.

John picks up the story in his Gospel in chapter 21.[1] We find Peter doing what he did best: fishing. He had gone out, probably to think things over with some of the other disciples. They had caught nothing when Jesus appeared to them on the shore and told them to throw their nets to the other side of the boat. This was not the first time He had said something like this (see Luke 5). Once again, they caught so many fish that they were unable to bring them aboard. John realized that it was Jesus and acknowledged this fact (John 21:7). Peter was so excited to know this he jumped into the water with all of his clothes on.

When Peter arrived at the shore, Jesus was cooking some fish. I think that Peter's excitement might have died away as he realized that he now had to face Jesus. The thrill of seeing Jesus melted into a sick dread of what Jesus might say. How would He react to Peter after his great failure? We too must wonder what He would say to us after we have let Him down.

Jesus simply pointed Peter back to the main issue. After serving the meal, Jesus asked Peter, "Simon son of John, do you truly love me more than these?" We don't know to

---

[1] The following is not meant to be a complete exegesis of John 21. There are many details and nuances that this summary cannot pursue. If the reader would like a detailed description of the passage, Leon Morris' excellent work, *The Gospel According to John* in the New International Commentary of the New Testament is recommended.

what "these" was referring. Jesus could have meant, "Do you love me more than these men love me?" Or he could have meant, "Do you love me more than you love these men?" Or "Do you love me more than these things?" It is not possible to know exactly, but however He intended the statement, Jesus was pressing Peter to examine his love for Him. How much did Peter love Jesus? It was a reminder of the Greatest Commandment.

Peter answered Jesus by telling Him the equivalent of, "Of course Jesus. You know that I love You." Jesus then helped Peter apply that love by saying, "Feed my sheep." Jesus wanted Peter to take care of the ones who were following Him. Jesus went on to ask His question ("Do you love me?") two more times. Peter became distressed and reminded Jesus, "Lord, you know all things; you know that I love you" (John 21:17). Now, if Jesus knew all things—and we know that He did and still does—why did Jesus keep asking Peter the question, "Do you love me?" Wasn't that a way to remind Peter about what was most important? Jesus' statements serve as a reminder to us that despite our sin and failures, the expectation from Jesus is that we will continue to love Him.

Jesus did not ask Peter to feel guilty or to do some sort of penance; He simply asked him about his love. Jesus told Peter this love would require him to go where he did not want to go and to die a death that he did not want to die. Jesus asked Peter to love Him and to make that love such a priority that he would become a martyr. The love of Jesus carries with it a great consequence. It will cause believers to go places that they normally would not go.

Peter's life was transformed. Where once there was a simple fisherman, there became a great leader of the church. During Jesus' trial, Peter was afraid to stand for Jesus. After Jesus was raised from the dead and ascended into heaven, Peter preached a sermon at which over three thousand people came to faith in Jesus Christ (Acts 2). The love of God changed him. It empowered him to do what God had created him to do.

And I want it to empower and change me. Do you want it to change you?

A while back I stumbled onto this idea: If loving God is the most important commandment, why don't I ask God to help me do it? I thought about the Scripture that says, "I tell you the truth, my Father will give you whatever you ask in my name" (John 16:23). What kind of prayer would God answer? It would be one in which I ask Him to cause me to obey His commandments. What if you asked Him to help you observe His Greatest Commandment? Wouldn't God want you to pray that? I think that He would.

So I began to make it my discipline to pray the prayer, "God, help me to love You more." I prayed it every day. I offered it at the times when I felt myself being pulled to love the things of the world. When I began to feel sorry for myself, I asked God to channel this love of self back to a love of Him. When I felt alone, I prayed the prayer. In times of fear, my prayer reminded me that, "There is no fear in love. But perfect love drives out fear, because fear has to do with punishment. The one who fears is not made perfect in love"

(1 John 4:18). I even prayed it when things went well. We should love God more than the blessings and successes that He gives us. We must be on guard during the good times. It is then when we are most susceptible to temptation.

The prayer began to permeate my thinking. All my life I had heard Christians talk about the love of God and how their lives had been touched. I was sure that I had a relationship with the Creator and was being transformed by Him, but I wanted to actually *experience* the love of God. I had the head knowledge of God and I knew that He loved me, but now I wanted to love Him back. I wanted the Greatest Commandment to come alive in my life. I truly wanted to love God wholeheartedly. I wanted to love God more than I loved the things of the world. My prayer reflected my deepest desire. God began to answer my prayer and I found that I had a growing desire to love Him. I worried less about what others thought of me, less about my financial problems, and less about the amount of prestige that I was or was not accumulating in this world.

I started asking myself why I love this world so much. What makes me hold on to it when I know that it won't last? We are all heading to an eternity with or without God, so I do not understand why we all hold on to this world and its riches so tightly. It is the same as holding on to your armrests in an airplane when you become afraid. Do you believe that the seat will not go down if the plane does? What are you thinking? So why hold on to the things of this world that will be destroyed with the rest of the world? Paul tells us in Colossians:

> Since, then, you have been raised with Christ, set your hearts on things above, where Christ is seated at the right hand of God. Set your minds on things above, not on earthly things. For you died, and your life is now hidden with Christ in God. When Christ, who is your life, appears, then you also will appear with him in glory.
>
> —COLOSSIANS 3:1–4

Over and over Scripture tells us to not love the world. Paul states that we are to set our hearts and minds on things above. He reminds me that I will appear with God in glory. I have the words of Jesus when He commands me not to worry about what I wear or what I eat (Matthew 6:25–34). But I still *do* worry about the things of this world. It is a matter of what I love the most. I want to love God, but I wind up loving the things that I can see and the things that other people tell me that I should love.

It will not be a resolute mind that tears one away from the love of the world. It will be a love for God that *He* plants in the heart and mind. If you want to make that significant change that will reorder your priorities, then you need to get on your knees today and ask God to help you love Him more. Ask Him fervently to give you a new heart and mind that will pursue the Love of your life. Tell God that you want to return, in a small way, the great love that He has expressed to you. We must be urgent in our prayer. It is His greatest commandment that we are trying to obey.

Do not wait until later to pray the prayer. If there is the smallest desire in you to love God, ask Him to cause that desire to grow. Make it your daily discipline to pray, "God help me to love you more." Ask God for the heart, soul, mind, and strength to love Him. Your life will never be the same. Go ahead. Do it right now. We are all waiting.

And so is He.

Discussion Questions

1. What do people ask God to give them? About what do people normally pray?

2. In your opinion, what kind of prayers would God like to hear and answer?

3. Why do you think Peter went back to fishing after Jesus' death and resurrection? Where would you go if you thought that Jesus was gravely disappointed in you?

4. To what was Jesus referring with His question in John 22, "Do you love me more than these?" What might "these" be for us?

5. What reasons could someone give in order to not pray the prayer, "God, help me love You more"?

Chapter Six

The Result of Loving God

St. Augustine said, "Love God, then do what you please."
For when you have learned to love, you will not even
desire to do those things that might offend the One you
love.[1]

—MADAME GUYON

For Christ's love compels us, because we are convinced
that one died for all, and therefore all died. And he
died for all, that those who live should no longer live
for themselves but for him who died for them and was
raised again.

—2 CORINTHIANS 5:14–15

DID YOU DO it? You know . . . pray the prayer? I said, "Do
not put it off," so I hope that you didn't. If you did not ask
God to give you a greater love for Him, I challenge you to
do it now. If we really believe that Jesus was serious when
He issued the Great Commandment, then we should all be
asking God to give us the ability to obey it. As followers
of Christ, we should desperately desire to pursue Him in

---

[1] Madame Guyon, *Experiencing the Depths of Jesus Christ*
(Seedflowers, Jacksonville, Florida, 1975), p. 47.

the manner in which He asked. Jesus said to love God completely and we should give all we have in that endeavor.

What will happen when we begin to pray that prayer? Before we start, we must remember that God Himself is our only motivation for loving Him. We do not pray the prayer to get God to give us a red Cadillac or help us win the lottery. Our goal should be to love God because He is the most worthy focus of our love. We love Him because He is God and our Creator. Bernard of Clairvaux said, "The reason for loving God is God Himself; the way is to love Him beyond measure."[2] We are confronted with a God who is so great and magnificent that we are left with no alternative but to love Him. We do not seek Him for any other reward other than that of knowing and loving Him.

That having been said, once we begin to love God, through His power and motivation, we will begin to experience some changes in our life. We will become transformed in our thinking as we pursue the Creator. Our reward is God Himself; however, there will be results and blessings that we experience because of the growing love that we have for our God.

Result #1: The love of God compels believers to want to know Him and to obey Him

Paul told the Corinthians that, ". . . Christ's love compels us, because we are convinced that one died for all, and

---

[2] St. Bernard of Clairvaux, *On the Love of God and Other Selected Writings*, ed. Charles J. Dollen (Alba House, New York, New York, 1996), p. 3.

therefore all died" (2 Corinthians 5:14). The love of God, which God Himself bestows upon us, serves to convince us that Christ died for us. This compels us to act. We are driven to seek out the will of God. Because God loves us, we want to love Him back.

We take up our cross as Jesus commanded us in Matthew 16:24; not out of duty or guilt, but out of a deep desire to know this One who came to earth and gave His life that we might live. How far this is from the legalistic religions of the day, which teach that we must do certain things in order to be right with God. We are not trying to impress God by what we do, but we are reacting to His love for us. We are led by a God who came and who died a brutal death in order that we might truly know Him. God commands us to "pick up your cross and follow me," but only *after* He picked up *His* cross and led the way. It is His love that draws me.

Paul described his desire to follow after the crucified life of Jesus. In the letter to the Galatians, he said, "I have been crucified with Christ and I no longer live, but Christ lives in me. The life I live in the body, I live by faith in the Son of God, who loved me and gave himself for me" (Galatians 2:20). The great love of God calls the followers of Christ to leave their own agendas and to carry out His purposes. They "die" to their desires and "live" to the will of God. It is only in the love of God that this transformation will occur. Love is the great motivator, and no love drives us like the love of God.

We are also compelled by the love of God in our worship. This activity is changed as we are transformed by His

love. We will find ourselves sincerely participating in orga-
nized worship as we contemplate the love of God. Not too
long ago, as I attended a worship service, I became aware
that I was truly trying to sing to God and to honor Him in
my song. I had prayed that God would help me love Him
more and that I would learn to worship Him in a way in
which He would be pleased. As I sang, I was conscious that
I was, in fact, worshipping God. I was not worried about
our post-church activities. I did not read the bulletin as I
sang. I was just simply engaged with God, and I knew that
He had compelled me to do so. The desire to love and know
God overwhelmed me. Worship should be the time that we
allow ourselves to be given over to that great love of God.
As we experience those times when it happens, our lives are
changed.

Result #2: Fear is no longer a motivation

The things that we fear control us. We are constantly
concerned that we, or our loved ones, will be injured. We
are afraid that we will lose all of our money. Our need for
comfort is so great that it scares us that someday we might
not be comfortable. These fears, and those like them, produce people who live a life of worry and anxiety. We think
that God will not give us what we need to have a fulfilling
life. As we come to love God more, we no longer continually
ask for things that would make our lives more comfortable
(now I only do it *sometimes*). Captured by His love, we will
find ourselves praying for the same things for which Jesus
would pray. Jesus asked for God's will and for others that

needed God's healing (see Mark 1, Luke 22:31, and Matthew 26:31–46).

Are you the kind who wakes up in the middle of the night just so you can worry about your business? Do you find yourself tossing and turning, as you fear events that, most likely, will never happen? Here's something that you can "fret" about the next time that you are up at 2:00 A.M. Start being concerned about how you love God. Start to become obsessed with your desire to love Him more (yes, I said "obsessed"). As you long for His love, the prayer, "God, help me to love You more," will start to become ingrained in your thinking, and you will find yourself thinking about it more and more. You may also find yourself sleeping all night. The events you worried about earlier will not matter to you near as much as they used to.

Instead of worrying about business or the stock market, just pray the prayer, "God help me to love You more." Pray like your life depended on it (it actually does). Ask God to help you love Him more than you love your bonus. Or more than you love your hobby on which you spend all of your spare time and income. Ask God to replace your devotion to whatever dominates your thinking with a stronger love of Him.

Our fear extends to our families. How many of us are frozen in worry for the safety of our family? I am. Maybe we are just concerned that they get the right job or get into the right school. We might be worried that they will be injured or harmed. So we become fixated on our loved ones. When our faith is grounded in God's love, we will trust God with our families. The same loving God who came and died for us will also see that His will is carried out in our family members. We can trust Him and we will trust Him more as we love Him more.

Another sign of decreasing fear is that outcomes no longer drive us as they once did. John, in his discussion of love in 1 John 4:18, says, "There is no fear in love. But perfect love drives out fear, because fear has to do with punishment. The one who fears is not made perfect in love." Since we are not afraid of consequences, we no longer live with fear (or at least as much as we used to). We are not worried about losing our jobs since we know that in His perfect love for us, God will provide for us. We do not have to be concerned about impressing people anymore because we know that the Creator of the Universe loves us. We are now working toward the love of a God who does not need to be convinced to care for us. His love is much better than the love of people who might be tempted to desert us if we do not behave as they want. Invest in the permanent. Focus on the love of God more than the love of a fickle world.

Result #3: The love of neighbor emerges from our love of God

The Great Commandment came with its own application embedded in it. After Jesus gave the challenge to love God with the whole self, He said, "The second is this: 'Love your neighbor as yourself'" (Mark 28:31). Therein lies a great result of loving God. It is the love of our neighbor as well as a proper love of self. Many want to rush past the first commandment to love God in order to get to "love your neighbor as yourself." Yet, it is only after one has applied the first command into one's life that the second part of the Great Commandment can be acted upon. The love of God is what allows one to realize the second piece. Love God first, and then the love of neighbor will become possible.

As we are filled with God's love, we will start to think in the way He designed us. We will see those around us as people who were created by God and were made in His image. We will see them as cherished by God, and because we love Him, we will care about those whom He created. As we are reminded that the members of our churches are people for whom Christ died, we will find that we have a new appreciation for these neighbors.

This love will also be extended to those whom we do not even know. As Christ's church, we are called to a ministry of reconciliation (2 Corinthians 5:18). We will find ourselves out in our communities representing Christ (2 Corinthians 5:20) and will be doing the things that He would do if He were here in bodily form today. We are called to the strangers on the street in order to represent Christ to them. As Christians in today's world, we are led to the shelters, community centers, and any other place where Christ's presence is needed. It will only be through the miracle of Christ's love that we will be moved to leave our comfort zones in search of those in need of the healing power of God.

A proper view of God will enable us to love others, despite their lack of love for us. If we understand just a little of His great love for us, we will not be worried about how others love us. Rather, we will be free to love them and not expect to have that love returned. We are cherished by a God who does not need our love. Since we are created to be like Him, He can empower us to love others without expecting anything in return. It is hard to envision loving others for the simple reason that God loves them, but that is exactly our mission. We are so used to receiving something back on our investment that we believe the same is true for love. We invest money in order to get more money, but we love others because God asked us to do it. We are simply obeying His command to love those whom He created. The miracle is that we do receive love in return for ours, but we can never dictate how and when we will get it.

We can become like the Good Samaritan in Luke 10 who loved a man whom he did not know and invested funds that he knew would never be repaid. The teachers of the law couldn't imagine living a life like that. Jesus directed His story at the religious people who kept the law but knew little about the love of God. As Jesus related His story, He used a Samaritan man as the hero. These devout Jews would never love such a man, but it was he who did the godly thing. He cared for his fellow man. This man loved the victim of a crime in the same way he was loved by Jesus. In this parable of Jesus, the Samaritan is not mentioned again, and we are not told that he was given any satisfaction from this deed except that he did as God had commanded him. He loved his neighbor.

We, too, are called to love those around us in the same way that Jesus would if He were physically walking our streets today. I once heard that the greatest indication that we are being taken over by God's power is when we find ourselves loving people we do not even like. Maybe that's why Jesus told us to love our enemies and pray for those who persecute us (Matthew 5:44). When was the last time that you prayed for your enemy? Have you prayed lately for that person at the office who drives you crazy? The original prayer, "God, help me love You," may lead you to pray, "God help me love my colleagues who irritate me." You may find yourself loving the unlovable. "Love your neighbor" is not just a good idea, it is a result of loving God with all our heart, soul, mind, and strength. That love produces a deep desire to obey God when He calls on us to love others.

If you want to deeply experience God's love, begin to pray for those whom you dislike. Pick one person and ask God to give you love for that person. Quit hoping that they fail, but begin to pray that God would bless them. Pray for their families, their businesses, and their eternal life. You will experience as much change as they do. You will feel God's presence as you pray like Jesus would pray.

THERE ARE MANY other ways that the love of God will alter our lives. The fact is that the love of God will bring us to a closer relationship with Jesus. It is the glue that holds us together in community. It is the energy that makes us want to leave our comfort and seek out those whom God calls us to love. It is my strength in times of trouble. It is passion that causes me to want to change. It controls me and shapes me and defines me. Why wouldn't I want to ask for more of it?

When he was only one, our youngest son Chris was sitting in his high chair, eating his breakfast. In a moment when she was not thinking clearly, Suzie, my wife, handed him an open tube of lime yogurt. Instead of eating the yogurt, Chris began to swing the tube over his head. And of course he was holding the sealed end while the open end was free to fly around. Green yogurt went everywhere! We found specks of the gooey stuff all around his chair, on the curtains, on the ceiling and floor, in his ears, and even in the room adjacent to his chair. Everything was green! We found it for days. The tube had been emptied on all of his surroundings.

That is a picture of God's love within us. His great compassion should come flying out of us and land on all of those around us. We first focus on loving Him back. Then we see that His love cannot be contained and it finds its way to all of those with whom we come in contact. It spreads out from us and changes everything and everyone. This is love as it was meant to be. Do not fail to experience it for yourself.

Discussion Questions

1. How do you feel about Bernard of Clairvaux's statement, "The reason for loving God is God Himself; the way is to love Him beyond measure?"

2. How does the statement, "Pick up your cross and follow me" impact the average Christian?

3. Why is fear a motivator for our lives? How does fear keep us from loving and obeying God?

4. Why is there no fear in love? How does perfect love cast out fear? (See 1 John 4:18.)

5. Has God ever caused you to love someone that you did not like? What are the details of this experience? Have you ever asked God to help you love someone that you did not like? Why or why not?

Chapter Seven

Obey God

"If you love me, you will obey what I command."
—JOHN 14:15

"And the second is like it: 'Love your neighbor as yourself.' All the Law and the Prophets hang on these two commandments."
—MATTHEW 22:39–40

Observe the commands of the LORD your God, walking in his ways and revering him. For the LORD your God is bringing you into a good land—a land with streams and pools of water, with springs flowing in the valleys and hills; a land with wheat and barley, vines and fig trees, pomegranates, olive oil and honey; a land where bread will not be scarce and you will lack nothing; a land where the rocks are iron and you can dig copper out of the hills.
—DEUTERONOMY 8:6–9

WHEN WE GO to my hometown of Tyler to see my father, we almost always go to a certain Mexican restaurant. It has great food and we love to go there. If I did not know about this place, how would I know if it were good just by driving by? I could tell by how crowded it is. If I saw that the parking lot was full (and it always is) and that there is a long line waiting to get a table (and there always is), I would know that obviously a large number of people like to eat there.

Unless they were giving away free food (and they weren't!), I would take the large crowd to mean that this was a great place to eat. Once, we were in a hurry and did not want to wait so we went to another restaurant which was just down the road. There was no line there and we figured that we could save some time. As we ate, we were immediately reminded why we should have stayed at our favorite restaurant. The fact that no one was waiting at Brand X restaurant was a testimony to its mediocrity. We learned our lesson and from then on were quite willing to wait in line. So how do I know that a restaurant is good? I look for a long line. I find the parking lot that is the most crowded in town, and I have probably found the best restaurant. The line and the filled parking lot are the visible indications of a great place to eat. The food must be worth waiting for.

How do I know I love God? Remembering our thinking from the paragraph above, what serves as my greatest sign that I am beginning to love God more? If someone merely observed me, what would be the best indicator of my love for God? *It is my desire to obey God.* Obedience is the visible indication of my love for God.

Jesus said the following:

> "If anyone loves me, he will obey my teaching. My Father will love him, and we will come to him and make our home with him. He who does not love me will not obey my teaching. These words you hear are not my own; they belong to the Father who sent me."
>
> —JOHN 14:23–24

We come to understand the presence of God's love in us when we do what He says. My obedience is the best indicator of how I love God. If I want to measure my progress in loving God, I should look at how much I want to do what Scripture says. A maturing Christian will be one who progressively wants to obey God more and more.

As I began to write this book, a friend of mine told me, "You just can't pray to love God. You have to *do* something." He was concerned that I would advocate that Christians should only pray for God's love but not actually do anything. He was partly right. We *should* encourage the people of God to be men and women of action. They should be doing things that reflect the love of God. But my friend also missed a major point. When we ask God to help us love Him, God will strengthen our desire to obey and please Him. *We will begin to want to do what He wants us to do.* We are empowered by the Holy Spirit, the Presence of God. We will not have to focus on the "do." This is not about gritting our teeth and going out to obey God, whether we like it or not. God will transform us to become people of obedience. Jesus left us the mighty Counselor to enable us to do His will. Jesus told the disciples:

> "And I will ask the Father, and he will give you another Counselor to be with you forever—the Spirit of truth. The world cannot accept him, because it neither sees him nor knows him. But you know him, for he lives with you and will be in you."
>
> —JOHN 14:16–17

My priorities will become the same as God's. My "doings" will reflect my relationship with God. My motivation will be changed and I will find myself wanting to carry out the orders of God. What I "do" is obey God.

We can actually experience our love for God and neighbor lived out in our life. John said that we love the children of God by obeying God. Jesus applied the Great Commandment (love God with all one's being) when He said that we were to love our neighbor as ourselves. It is a call to obedience. Jesus wants His followers to mirror His heart in their daily actions. This obedience will encourage His children.

Here's how John put it:

> This is how we know that we love the children of God: by loving God and carrying out his commands. This is love for God: to obey his commands. And his commands are not burdensome, for everyone born of God overcomes the world. This is the victory that has overcome the world, even our faith.
>
> —1 JOHN 5:2–4

As I do what God asks me to, I will find that it benefits the children of God. I do not run into their cars as I speed down the freeway, because God tells me to obey the law. I can even love my family more by obeying God! God tells me not to exasperate my children in Ephesians 6:4; and in Ephesians 5:25 and 1 Corinthians 13 He gives me ideas on how to love my wife. If I would obey those passages, my family would be better able to experience God's love. I take care of God's people when I obey His commands. God's orders are designed to protect others, as well as me. We can become great lovers of God's people when we just do what God asks us to do!

Author David Watson in his book *Called and Committed* (I highly recommend that book if you can find a copy) summarizes the above points:

> This call of Jesus to his disciples was also a call of love. Their obedience to his Word meant trusting in his love. It is because Jesus loves us and has laid down his life for us that he looks for a total response of love on our part, a love whose reality is tested by obedience. Do we really want to be his disciples? Do we genuinely want God's perfect will for our lives? Are we honestly willing to trust ourselves to One who demands all, but who loves us more than anyone could ever love us and who longs only for our highest good? The test must be unquestioning obedience to his Word. If we reject his Word, we question his wisdom and doubt his love, and we cannot be his disciples.[1]

Jesus calls us to obey the Father just as He did. Jesus wants us to live the kind of life He did. He said, "The world must learn that I love the Father and that I do exactly what my Father has commanded me" (John 14:31). The greatest leaders are those who never ask any of their followers to do what they themselves are unwilling to do. Many managers instruct their employees to perform certain tasks that they

---

[1] David Watson, *Called and Committed: World-Changing Discipleship* (Harold Shaw Publishers, Wheaton, Illinois, 1982), p. 176.

themselves would not do. Who wants to follow someone like that? But Jesus issued His commands in John 14 in anticipation that He Himself would lead the way in obeying God, the Father.

We recently took a family vacation to Washington, D.C. Most people who go there are reminded of the roots of our country and the sacrifices that have been given for our freedoms. These sacrifices take many forms, but it is the giving of life that most gets our attention as we tour that city. From the Vietnam Memorial, the Law Enforcement Memorial, the Tomb of the Unknown Soldier, the World War II Memorial, and many others, we are touched by the lives that have been given in the service of our country. Walk through Arlington Cemetery and you cannot help but wonder how this immense debt can ever be repaid. A tour of any battlefield on which American forces have fought gives one a feeling of supreme gratitude. You are left with a desire to give a sacrifice to the country for which those people died.

In a letter to his son, General Robert E. Lee exhorted him, "Do your duty in all things. You cannot do more. You should never wish to do less." Should we, as Christians, not have that same attitude? Why do we pay tribute to those who give their lives in defense of our country and not with equal *or greater* gratitude honor those who give their lives in their obedience to God?

Some of these Christian heroes have given their lives away on God's behalf. The lives of St. Augustine, Hudson Taylor, Billy Graham, Jim Elliott, Elisabeth Elliott, and countless others remind us that many before us have made great sacrifices—some even unto death—as they followed Jesus Christ.

Now come take a "walk" through Hebrews 11. Find a Bible and turn to that passage. Here we have a scene which is similar to that found at Arlington Cemetery, except that the sacrifices made here are to a far greater cause than those made by our American heroes. As you browse this chapter of the Bible, you see Abraham, Isaac, Noah, Joseph, and Moses, just to mention a few. You will find those who followed God in faith even though they faced arduous experiences.

> Others were tortured and refused to be released, so that they might gain a better resurrection. Some faced jeers and flogging, while still others were chained and put in prison. They were stoned; they were sawed in two; they were put to death by the sword. They went about in sheepskins and goatskins, destitute, persecuted and mistreated—the world was not worthy of them. They wandered in deserts and mountains, and in caves and holes in the ground.
>
> —HEBREWS 11:35–38

This is the "great cloud of witnesses" to which Hebrews 12:1 refers. But what does this mean? It means that you are not alone! You have been preceded by thousands of men and women who, with all the strength that they had, pursued the God of Scripture and sought to obey Him. Our call today is to join those who have gone before us and have given us a model (yes, an imperfect model) of what obeying God looks like. All of those suffering heroes mentioned in Hebrews 11 are now cheering you on! As you attempt to fight through your life, this cloud of ancient brothers and sisters roots for you from their eternal home in heaven. After the writer has reminded his readers of the many heroes of the faith in chapter 11, he provides a great charge in the opening of chapter 12:

> Therefore, since we are surrounded by such a great cloud of witnesses, let us throw off everything that hinders and the sin that so easily entangles, and let us run with perseverance the race marked out for us. Let us fix our eyes on Jesus, the author and perfecter of our faith, who for the joy set before him endured the cross, scorning its shame, and sat down at the right hand of the throne of God. Consider him who endured such opposition from sinful men, so that you will not grow weary and lose heart.
>
> —HEBREWS 12:1–3

We are surrounded by a great group of experienced travelers, who loved and obeyed God with all they had. The writer tells his readers to throw off whatever hinders them in their life with Christ and to leave the sins that entangle them. He urges them to run the race, their life calling, with perseverance. Our motivation to obey is grounded in Jesus who now sits at the right hand of God having called us to the same battle that He fought while He was on earth.

In order to remind ourselves of the fight that our Savior fought, we switch scenes once more. We now find ourselves in a small garden near Jerusalem about two thousand years ago. One lone figure is seen kneeling and praying to His Father. He was in such agony that His sweat fell like great drops of blood. There, Jesus experienced the greatest challenge that has ever been or ever will be faced. Matthew 26:39 states, "Going a little farther, he fell with his face to the ground and prayed, 'My Father, if it is possible, may this cup be taken from me. Yet not as I will, but as you will.'" If you want to talk about sacrifice, here is the perfect model. Here is Jesus asking the Father for another way to save the world, but in the same breath, vowing to obey God even if it meant death. The person who chooses to follow after Jesus must face this scene and ask the question, "What may be required of *me*?" We must obey the One who cried out in the garden and then simply did what He was told. There is no replacement for simple obedience in the Christian life. We are told to live our lives in faith. This faith is borne out as we follow Christ and obey as He obeyed.

The movie "Saving Private Ryan" is one of the most powerful films I have ever seen. Toward the end of the story, the hero, played by Tom Hanks, lays dying due to injuries sustained in saving James Francis Ryan, a private. He looks at Matt Damon, who played Private Ryan, and says the words, "Earn this; earn this." In the final scene, the now middle-aged Ryan finds himself in France at the Normandy Beach cemetery. He is staring at the grave of the captain (Hanks' character) who rescued him. As his wife walks over to him, he tearfully asks her, "Am I a good man?" He wants to know if he "earned it." In asking, he speaks to all Americans who know they should live their lives in a way that memorializes the country's heroes whose lives bought for them this free country.

Fortunately, Jesus does NOT tell us to earn it. He simply calls us to accept this *gift* of life because *He* is the One who has earned it. The eternal life that was purchased for us on the cross is simply a gift to be received. We do not have to earn it, yet we are *called* to obey our sacrificed and risen Lord in all that we do out of gratitude for what He has already done. No matter what the cost. Not looking back to anything left behind for the sake of the gospel.

My friend that I mentioned at the first of this chapter was worried that I would simply pray a prayer and not do anything. My reply is that if I pray, "God, help me to love You," then God will direct me to *obey* Him. I cannot help but do what He wants me to do. "The love of God compels me" to obey Him (2 Corinthians 5:14). We simply obey our Creator, just like Jesus did. Just like the believers in Hebrews 11 did. Just like modern Christians heroes do everyday as they wade through this life.

I have friends in Houston who direct some great inner city ministries. Sometimes they are lonely and discouraged. Sometimes they are afraid that they will be harmed. Sometimes they run out of money and cannot be paid. But they always keep going. They do not quit. They obey God's call on their lives. They are my heroes. And so is the woman who takes her children to church every Sunday while her husband sleeps in. And so is the man who does his work honestly when it would be easier and more profitable to "cook the books." And so is the student who shares his or her faith with school friends when it might not be the fashionable thing to do. Perhaps those latter acts are not as dramatic as the inner city work, but they are nonetheless heroic.

In *The Church of Irresistible Influence*, Robert Lewis says:

> More than by decades or centuries, history is marked by great ideas; that is, when someone, placed in unique culture and circumstance, stands up and says, "What if we believed—and acted upon—this?"[2]

What if we believed and acted upon what we know to be true? What if we began to move in our world with the purpose that God has laid out for us in Scripture? It is about time that some men and women set about the simple yet most difficult task of obedience. Many of us already know what God wants us to do. It is not hard to see in the Bible that we are to love our neighbors, pray for our enemies, etc. These commands are hard because they go against what we really want to do, which is *our* will! It is indeed most difficult to obey the will of God. What will it take?

Discussion Questions

1. Why is obedience a good indicator of how much you love someone?

2. Why is it so hard to love your neighbor or those with whom you work, play, or worship? Take each category—work, play, and worship—and discuss how

---

[2] Robert Lewis, *The Church of Irresistible Influence* (Zondervan, Grand Rapids, Michigan, 2001), p. 55.

each one is different.

3. How can you tell if someone is maturing in his or her faith?

4. Who is one of your biblical heroes? Describe their love for God.

5. Are you encouraged or intimidated by your current Christian heroes? Why?

Chapter Eight

Obedience Takes Faith

Today there is no shortage of pious words, affirmations
of faith, discussions about hunger, or expressions
of spirituality. But the world is still waiting for the
demonstration, in hard, costly, and practical terms,
of what we glibly proclaim from our lips. Let it not
be that "I was hungry, and you formed a committee
to investigate my hunger . . . I was homeless, and
you filed a report on my plight . . . I was sick, and you
held a seminar on the underprivileged . . . You have
investigated my plight. And yet I am still hungry,
homeless, and sick.[1]

—DAVID WATSON

Do not merely listen to the word, and so deceive
yourselves. Do what it says. Anyone who listens to
the word but does not do what it says is like a man
who looks at his face in a mirror and, after looking at
himself, goes away and immediately forgets what he
looks like. But the man who looks intently into the
perfect law that gives freedom, and continues to do this,
not forgetting what he has heard, but doing it—he will
be blessed in what he does.

—JAMES 1:22–25

IF YOU HAVE ever played a sport, chances are good that you
had a coach. Why do we need that? It is because we need

---

[1] Watson, p. 160.

someone who has gone before us (hopefully) and can instruct us on how the sport should be played. When you have an expert coach (unlike me when I coached soccer or lacrosse), you have someone who understands the game and whose advice can make you play better. That is . . . if you do what they tell you to do.

I had the pleasure of coaching Little League baseball for nine years. The one thing I always tried to teach my team was to trust me and do what I told them. If I said "run," that was what they were supposed to do. I reminded them not to worry about the outcome of the play, just do what I said. I would take responsibility for the result of my decision. Their job was just to carry out my orders. I always told them, "Just let me be the coach." The ones who believed in my ability would follow my advice. Listen to this: The ones who had *faith* in me, as the coach, would do what I told them to do. Their actions became an evidence of their trust in me. And no matter what happened, they always got a snow cone in the end.

The above is an obvious illustration for us in the Christian life. Just do what God says to do. Just let Him be the Lord. Sometimes, we are afraid that we will "make an out." We worry that we might fail, or what's worse, that we might become uncomfortable. After all, what if God tells us to go to Africa or to the inner city? What if He asks us to quit a great paying job and move to a ministry? We might behave like some of my former ballplayers who wanted to make their own decisions as they ran the bases. When the going got tough or risky, they resisted my coaching and just did what felt right. If God calls us to difficult situations, we must obediently follow and trust Him for the results.

The point is clear. My faithful actions will be the result of my active faith. This faith will pour through my life and surface as obedience. James said faith without deeds is dead (James 2:26). God tells me through James that my desire to follow His commands will clearly evidence my belief. My obedience takes faith, which comes alive in what I do. These actions will be similar to what Jesus did when He was on earth. Paul said it like this:

> Your attitude should be the same as that of Christ Jesus:
>
> Who, being in very nature God, did not consider equality with God something to be grasped,
>
> but made himself nothing, taking the very nature of a servant, being made in human likeness.
>
> And being found in appearance as a man, he humbled himself and became obedient to death—even death on a cross!
>
> —PHILIPPIANS 2:5–8

Peter's words were, "To this you were called, because Christ suffered for you, leaving you an example, that you should follow in his steps" (1 Peter 2:21). Jesus, in Luke 6:46, clearly said, "Why do you call me, 'Lord, Lord,' and do not do what I say?" How can I claim to be a follower of Jesus and not obey Him? How can I say that I have faith if I am not willing to obey the One in whom I am supposed to have faith? Look at the thoughts of several writers:

Dietrich Bonhoeffer, a German pastor who stood up to

Adolf Hitler and was subsequently imprisoned and martyred for his faith during the Second World War:

> Only he who believes is obedient and only he who is obedient believes . . . for faith is only real when there is obedience, never without it, and faith only becomes faith in the act of obedience.[2]

Bill Hull, in his influential book, *The Complete Book of Discipleship*, says, "It is simply absurd to say that you believe, or even want to believe in him, if you do not do anything that he tells you."[3] Andrew Murray took it one step further with his thought, "He (Jesus) showed us that obedience is the eternal purpose of the Father. It is the great objective of the work of the Spirit and a chief part of the salvation of Christ."[4]

Did Paul, Peter, Bonhoeffer, and Jesus know what they were talking about when they discussed obedience? Absolutely. The first three, while they lived imperfect lives, gave their physical lives as evidence of their desire to follow Jesus, who gave His own life perfectly in the pursuit of obedience to His Father. Scripture calls us to be conformed to the likeness of Christ (Romans 8:29). This conformity can only come through the mysterious intersection of God's

---

[2] Dietrich Bonhoeffer, *The Cost of Discipleship* (MacMillan, New York, New York 1977), p. 69.

[3] Bill Hull, *The Complete Book of Discipleship* (NavPress, Colorado Springs, Colorado, 2006), p. 117.

[4] Andrew Murray, *The Blessings of Obedience* (Whitaker House, New Kensington, Pennsylvania, 1984), p. 19.

empowerment and our obedience. God calls me and then draws me to obey Him, yet there is room for me to act upon that call.

The writer of Hebrews draws our attention to the perfect model of Jesus. "Let us fix our eyes on Jesus, the author and perfecter of our faith, who for the joy set before him endured the cross, scorning its shame, and sat down at the right hand of the throne of God. Consider him who endured such opposition from sinful men, so that you will not grow weary and lose heart" (Hebrews 12:2-3). And again in Hebrews 5, the writer says, "Although he was a son, he learned obedience from what he suffered and, once made perfect, he became the source of eternal salvation for all who obey him" (Hebrews 5:8-9).

If even Jesus had to obey God without reservation, why do I think that I will not have to?

Andrew Murray points out, "Jesus came into the world for one purpose. He lived only to carry out God's will. The single, supreme, all-controlling power of His life was obedience."[5]

"The issue at point is crucial," Carl Wilson says, "the one that matters most."

> We do need more "decisions" in evangelism, more effective church management and organization, more money to run churches, and sometimes we may even need better buildings and facilities. But woe be to us as Christians

---

[5] Murray, p. 31.

if we do not see that the greatest need of the hour is to help Christians clearly understand and obey the teachings of Christ. We need to help Christians apply these to their daily lives and to teach them that obedience to His commands is of utmost importance.

Praying a prayer to invite Christ into one's heart, having an emotional experience, testifying for Christ, sharing the "plan of salvation," entering into the fullness of the Holy Spirit, teaching the Bible, and many other Christian acts are valid and good. But they mean nothing, *absolutely nothing*, unless they begin to produce the fruits of righteousness. While salvation is by grace through faith alone, faith without works is *dead*, nonexistent! (James 2:17). I believe that I have the mind of Christ when I say that if we have city-wide crusades with thousands of "decisions," hold huge Bible conferences and seminars with outstanding speakers, and enact programs of social and political justice for the poor, it all counts as *nothing* if Jesus is not obeyed in our private lives."[6]

"Agreement isn't enough," writes Bill Hull, "faith becomes real only when we obey. Obedience is the only worthy goal of Christian spirituality."[7] Obedience is necessary, yes even crucial, to our Christian faith. We are called into the kingdom of God through the life and death of Jesus Christ. In the lives of the apostles and in the early church,

---

[6] Carl F. Wilson, *With Christ in the School of Disciple Building* (Zondervan, Grand Rapids, Michigan, 1976), p.273.

[7] Hull, p. 134.

this life drove followers to become imitators of Christ. Today, we have traded this Kingdom call to a life of obedience into one of simply avoiding hell. Why do we evangelize? Many would probably say that it is because we do not want people to miss out on heaven when they die. But that is not what Jesus proposed to His first disciples. Yes, we should care desperately about the eternal destination of the souls of others. To care in such a way is consistent with the heart of God. Yet the call of Jesus to those He encountered was to *follow* Him and He would make them "fishers of men" on earth (Matthew 4:19)! Those who obediently pursued that invitation saw their lives transformed and the Kingdom advanced. The Christianity of the apostles was one of radical obedience. They gave their lives for their faith, just as their Lord did.

The obedience of the disciples was their "call." Jesus was their focal point and motivation. His commands transformed their knowledge of Him into a faith that would be seen by what they actually did. Their compliance pointed out that they believed He was their Lord. They proved their faith by following Him and conforming their wills to His. Without their obedience, there would be no evidence that they believed in Him. The truth was that they followed Him down the road and this was proof of their faith. Within the lives of the disciples Bonheoffer's statement is established, "Without obedience, there is no faith."

Jesus was obedient to death. He saw His mission through to the cross. Jesus submitted unto death because that was His calling. God calls every disciple to be obedient until death as well. This brings us face to face with Jesus' words, "If anyone would come after me, he must deny himself and take up his cross and follow me" (Matthew 16:24). What must we deny in order to follow in His footsteps? We must die to our will as we take up His cross for our lives.

What are you holding on to that keeps you from God's will? For me it's almost always my personal agenda. I want to preserve my time and my schedule. The need to be in control of my daily activities is overwhelming. Those of us who desperately attempt to maintain our life exactly as we want it will either completely miss the transformation of Christ or live a life of frustration as we refuse the commands of Jesus. Disciples must die a daily death that takes place hour after hour, day after day, week after week, month after month, until we draw our last breath. As we come to accept that lifestyle, we bring glory to God.

> God's glory will be seen in those who are prepared to accept the path of obedience, the way of the cross and the pain of relationships. That is how Jesus lived; setting His face like a flint, doing always what pleased the Father. As we follow Jesus this way we can bring salvation to the world.[8]

We need to become men and women who will put our actions where our mouths are. It is imperative for our faith that we reject the idea that Jesus *only* comes to save us from hell. He comes rather to implant in us His heart and desire

---

[8] Watson, p. 188.

to do the will of the Father. We will never grow in our faith until we trust His goodness by acting upon what we know to be true. We must discover that we *can* love our enemies. He *will* empower us to turn the other cheek. We *can* hold our tongue and honor God by not returning an insult. Our money truly *is* His and when we give beyond what we think is reasonable, we can test His faithfulness to us (Malachi 3:10). Jesus, in turn, "tests" our faith by placing tasks in front of us that will cause us to trust Him. David Watson says, "Jesus' aim in testing our obedience is to bring us to the point of genuine faith in him."[9]

What if the Christians of the world began to live out their faith? What if some of us actually turned down a job transfer in order to continue in a ministry to the homeless? If we have given our lives to Jesus Christ, then we must be different than those who do not follow Him. Our marriages must reflect a bold commitment to stay with the one whom God gave us as our lifelong partner. We must work out solutions to "irreconcilable differences." If God hates divorce, then we must constantly pray that we will also. Our work relationships must reflect an integrity that can come only from a total trust in the outcomes assigned by the Father. Our love of our neighbor, and yes, even our enemy, is driven by a simple, childlike faith in a God who promises us a complete life in Him that can be experienced through our obedience to Him.

We trust our eternal destiny to God through Jesus

---

[9] Watson, p. 178.

Christ, and we are happy to accept the salvation that He provides. We want the safety and security of heaven. We claim joy and peace that comes from knowing Him, yet we are scared to death that He might call us to go to China or even across town to those who are without hope. The idea that we might have to give up purchasing a new car in order to feed the hungry or clothe those who are freezing may seem like a foreign concept in even the best of Christian circles. How could God mean for us to reject a big promotion just so we could have more time to volunteer with a youth organization? Someone told us that the Christian life would make our life easier, but in truth, our lives are sometimes complicated by hard decisions that we now must make for the Kingdom. We feel like we should hold back and protect ourselves from a loving God who is calling us to abandon all and follow Him. We are, in fact, afraid to trust Him.

Where is our faith? How can we learn to trust a loving God with our lives? Why would we fear the life that He offers us? He has given us the greatest sacrifice that one could ever give. Scripture tells of some who have followed Him with all that they have. In the next chapter we will take a look at one of them.

Discussion Questions

1. Why do you agree or disagree with Bonheoffer's statement, "Only he who believes is obedient and only he who is obedient believes . . . for faith is only real when there is obedience, never without it, and faith only becomes faith in the act of obedience"?

2. When has your faith become real because you obeyed God when it would have been easier or more convenient not to?

3. What is the average Christian holding on to that keeps him from obeying God?

4. How does the definition of a hypocrite fit into a discussion of Christian obedience?

5. Why do some cling to the idea that Jesus came to make them comfortable on earth? How do you feel about the so-called "prosperity gospel"?

Chapter Nine

Obedience Requires The Word

> The LORD had said to Abram, "Leave your country, your people and your father's household and go to the land I will show you. I will make you into a great nation and I will bless you; I will make your name great, and you will be a blessing. I will bless those who bless you, and whoever curses you I will curse; and all peoples on earth will be blessed through you."
>
> So Abram left, as the LORD had told him; and Lot went with him. Abram was seventy-five years old when he set out from Haran. He took his wife Sarai, his nephew Lot, all the possessions they had accumulated and the people they had acquired in Haran, and they set out for the land of Canaan, and they arrived there.
>
> —GENESIS 12:1–5

ABRAHAM COULD WELL go down as one of the greatest "obeyers" in all of history. Who, at the age of seventy-five, would leave a great life in the fertile land beside the Euphrates River in order to go settle in a desert? Imagine that you are living in your dream house, with all of the servants, cattle, and produce that you could use. Your life is comfortable and all is well. The only problem is that you do not have a son who could inherit all of your possessions. But who can have it all? Life is good, so maybe you should just coast on in and enjoy retirement. Sound familiar? It is what every working man or woman in America hopes will be his or her fate.

God comes to you and asks you to leave all of your comfort and move. What would you say? You would probably ask, "OK, God, where do you want me to move? And by the way, what do you want me to do when I get there? What kind of salary will be available? Is there a stock option plan in this deal?" God answers only that He wants you to leave your country, your parents, and your friends. Leave everything that you know and go to a place that He will show you later. Most of us would probably thank God for showing us His will and then ask if there was another will that He could give us instead. Is there such a thing as Will #2? *What else do you have for me God?*

There were so many things that could go wrong. Abraham had so much to lose. Yet, Abraham did have one sure thing. *He had God's audible Word.* There was no question as to what God wanted him to do. He knew the proposition God was presenting because he had heard Him say it out loud.

In America, we understand "the deal." Most of us love to make a good deal. We make our case by saying, "You do this and I will do that. You pay me and I will deliver." God now presented "the big deal" to Abraham. God asked him to go to a land to be revealed later. Because of his obedience, God would bless Abraham by making him a leader of a great nation. God would bless those who blessed him and curse those who cursed him. All that Abraham had to do was to leave all that he treasured, and obey God. Now, again, what would *you* have done?

Our greatest problem in the Christian life is not that we do not know the will of God. It is that we *do* know it and are not willing to obey it! That "great theologian" Mark Twain said, "It ain't the parts of the Bible that I can't understand that bother me, it is the parts that I do understand." I do not agree much with what Mark Twain said about God and the Bible, but I do resonate with that statement. We constantly look for the clear and easy way to follow Christ. Maybe we should realize that the way is clear, but sometimes it "ain't" that easy. It is simple, yet may be extremely difficult. Sometimes we may say, "If God would just come down and tell me what to do, I would do it." Oh, really? God came down and told Abraham. Would you have done what he did? God also speaks to us daily in the Scriptures. How are we doing with that?

Does the knowledge that God's will appears on every page of Scripture cause us to become men and women of the Word? The idea that God speaks through His living Word should drive us to the Bible. One who reads the Scripture should do so with the goal of wanting to know what God wants for him or her. Why aren't Christians combing passages of Scripture in order to determine what to do next? Pastors and teachers declare that God speaks directly through Scripture and there He gives instructions for His people to live. Yet when Christians are asked to spend a mere five minutes a day reading the Bible, they turn down the invitation in droves. Call me crazy, but I do not think that makes good sense. We need to learn more about following God.

There are two ingredients in obedience. The first is the command; I must know what I am supposed to do. Nothing happens until I am told what to do. When we begin a job, we generally are taken on a tour of the office and shown the important places (coffee room, restroom, etc.). Then we might sit down with our new boss in order to be given our responsibilities. We take a job assuming that our supervisor will tell us what we are supposed to do. Can you imagine being a good employee without having someone tell you what the job is? Step one of being a good follower is having a good set of instructions to follow.

Second in the process of obedience is having a willingness to do what is required. You can be told what to do, but if you don't intend to comply, why should someone bother to tell you? One should want to follow the desires of an employer. Try this experiment next week at work: When your boss assigns you a task, just say no. If he questions your answer, tell him, "I just don't feel like it." Then, as you begin to look for a new job, you will understand the need to make the commitment that your will should be that of your employer. Likewise, one needs a heart and mind to do what God wants done. Any good follower has the capacity to seek and then *do* what his leader asks of him.

Something interesting happens when someone really loves his job. He begins to do *more* than he is asked. The mark of a fulfilling job is when the employee has to be reminded to go home. The worker constantly seeks out additional work because he or she wants the company to do well. He likes his employers and therefore wants to make them happy and successful. His love of the company is his motivator. He earnestly desires to make the boss happy and works to do so.

I love my wife. I try to do what she asks because I want to make her happy. Sometimes, I may actually ask her what she would like me to do, and then, I go do it. I might even go out of my way to complete a task that I know she wants done yet hasn't asked me to do . . . (I did not say that I do this all the time). It is not the pay that drives me. It is my love for my wife that makes me want to obey her wishes. Pleasing her is my heart's desire.

What happens when we love God? Remember? We do what He commands. But we do not just sit back and hope that we will magically know what He wants. We actually search for His will. We go to Scripture and find His commands. We let the Bible tell us what we are to do. We do not just read it in order to be good historians or experts on the literature of Scripture. *Christians study the Bible in order to know their job.* We come to love what the Bible says because we love its Author. Why else would the psalmist say, "Oh, how I love your law! I meditate on it all day long" (Psalm 119:97)? Why did the psalmist meditate on the Word all day long? In order to do what the beloved Author commanded!

James reminds us about the importance of obedience to the Word when he says,

> Do not merely listen to the Word, and so deceive your-
> selves. Do what it says. Anyone who listens to the Word
> but does not do what it says is like a man who looks at
> his face in a mirror and, after looking at himself, goes
> away and immediately forgets what he looks like. But the
> man who looks intently into the perfect law that gives
> freedom, and continues to do this, not forgetting what
> he has heard, but doing it—he will be blessed in what
> he does.
>
> —JAMES 1:22–25

"The perfect law that gives freedom." Did you see that? We think that a law is something that takes away our freedom. Speed limit signs do. "No talking in the library" signs keep us from speaking when we want. But God's law gives us freedom. Within Scripture, we are told who we are supposed to be and what we are called to do. Who does not want that? How can we say, "If God would just come down here and speak to me," when He *has* come here in Jesus Christ? He now *remains* here in His Word and through His Holy Spirit. He will tell us what we are to do within the confines of Scripture. God has definitely communicated clearly. Armed with His presence and empowerment, it is up to Christians to believe and obey His Word. Listen to what the opening questions of the Shorter Catechism say:

> Q. 1. *What is the chief end of man?*
> A. Man's chief end is to glorify God, and to enjoy him forever.
>
> Q. 2. *What rule hath God given to direct us how we may glorify and enjoy him?*

A. The Word of God, which is contained in the Scriptures of the Old and New Testaments, is the only rule to direct us how we may glorify and enjoy him.

Q. 3. What do the Scriptures principally teach?
A. The Scriptures principally teach what man is to believe concerning God, and what duty God requires of man.

The early Christian fathers who penned these questions understood that the Word was the only place to go in order to properly understand faith and obedience. Their words tell me that Job #1 is to glorify God and enjoy Him forever. In order to do that, one must be directed by the Word that teaches what to believe and do. Does one's love for God cause him to go to Scripture and try to find out what He wants him to do? James Boice put it like this:

> If the adventure of discipleship involves obedience to Jesus Christ, as it certainly does, and if Jesus exercises His lordship over us so that we can obey Him through the Bible, as we have seen to be the case, then there can be no real discipleship apart from Bible study . . . Bible study is the most essential ingredient in the believer's spiritual life.[1]

Boice states that Bible study is "the most essential ingredient in the believer's spiritual life." It would not be out of order, then, to say that the believer needs the Bible in order to grow. The Word presents the will of God. It tells the believer what to do. The first stage of growth occurs as the

---

[1] James Montgomery Boice, *Christ's Call to Discipleship* (Moody Press, Chicago, Illinois, 1986), p. 52.

believer begins to pursue the Word in order to know what God wants. The second stage continues as one actually does what Scripture says. To be a follower of Christ, one must be willing to go to Scripture in order to know what His will is. How could one live the Christian life without that ingredient? Boice was right—Bible study is essential.

One Christmas, my mother gave our children a toy Jeep that they could drive around the yard. The instructions said that it would take me about one hour to put it together. That might have been true if I was a mechanical engineer. Otherwise, the instructions should have told me that it might take the average person, say, around four hours to complete the task . . . on Christmas Eve . . . while everyone else got to listen to the West Point Choir and watch Midnight Mass from the Vatican! It took me so long because I kept guessing what the next step was. I would not stay within the guidelines of the instruction book (note that I didn't say "booklet"—it was easily the size of a small encyclopedia). I finally learned, around 11:00 P.M., that I should just stick with the steps described in the book. I was tired of trying to do things my way, and I went with the manufacturer. Someone once said, "When all else fails, read the instructions." I would have punched "someone" in the nose if that had been said to me that wonderful Christmas Eve. By the way, why *do* you think those instructions were included in the box? I wonder . . .

Why do we think that God gave us His active Word? He wanted to reveal to us who He is and what He wants from us. In Scripture, God gives us everything we need for life and godliness (2 Peter 1:3). So shouldn't we begin to read the Word, not just for information, but also for a plan of attack on life? Jesus once asked His followers why they did not obey Him.

> "Why do you call me, 'Lord, Lord,' and do not do what I say? I will show you what he is like who comes to me and hears my words and puts them into practice. He is like a man building a house, who dug down deep and laid the foundation on rock. When a flood came, the torrent struck that house but could not shake it, because it was well built. But the one who hears my words and does not put them into practice is like a man who built a house on the ground without a foundation. The moment the torrent struck that house, it collapsed and its destruction was complete."
>
> —LUKE 6:46–49

The obeyed Word is like a rock. Jesus planted in the minds of His followers the picture of a strong base that could withstand a great storm. He compared disobedience to a house built on sand. When the bad times came, the house fell down.

In 2008, the cities of Galveston and Houston experienced Hurricane Ike. The people there can tell you about a bad storm. As tough as it was in Houston (where I live), it was ten times worse in Galveston. Entire homes were washed from the beach. The sand was sucked out to sea and anything that rested on top went with it. Jesus reminds us that His Word will not wash away. The obeyed Word will stand like a rock. It is solid and can hold up to any storm of

life, *if it is obeyed*! The Word that is heard and *not* obeyed
is like building a house on sand. How badly do you want to
obey the Word? We must obey if we desire to follow God.
James Boice said, "Jesus cannot be our Lord without obedience; and if He is not our Lord, we do not belong to Him.
We are like a man whose house will be swept away by a
flood."[2]

Now look at the opening words of the Psalms:

> Blessed is the man
>> who does not walk in the counsel of the wicked
>> or stand in the way of sinners
>> or sit in the seat of mockers.
>
> But his delight is in the law of the LORD,
>> and on his law he meditates day and night.
>
> He is like a tree planted by streams of water,
>> which yields its fruit in season
>> and whose leaf does not wither.
>> Whatever he does prospers.
>
> —PSALM 1:1–3

Here we read that the obeyed Word is like a tree planted by a stream. Ever been in the desert and seen what a
stream does to the land? Even if you have not walked in
that scorching environment, you know what happens. The
water that runs through the barren land begins to nour-
ish it and causes plants to grow. An oasis develops and becomes a place where plants and animals thrive. It becomes

---

[2] Boice, p. 49.

a beautiful jewel amidst the ugliness of the desert. What a picture! The obeyed Word is like that for us. It gives us life. It takes the dry and dead and causes it to live. The dust storm of our life is transformed into a place that others can come and find thirst quenching life. It is real and it is active. Why do we let ourselves miss it?

We will let the apostle Peter summarize our thoughts:

> Now that you have purified yourselves by obeying the truth so that you have sincere love for your brothers, love one another deeply, from the heart. For you have been born again, not of perishable seed, but of imperishable, through the living and enduring word of God. For,
> "All men are like grass,
> and all their glory is like the flowers of the field;
> the grass withers and the flowers fall,
> but the word of the Lord stands forever."
> And this is the word that was preached to you.
>
> —1 PETER 1:24–25

Discussion Questions

1. Would you rather hear God's audible voice, like Abraham, or have God's written Word as we have it now? Explain.

2. What are the reasons that we should study and know the Bible?

3. Describe how loving a job has caused you or

someone else to work harder than was really necessary. How can you apply that reasoning to the Christian life?

4. According to the Shorter Catechism, what do the Scriptures primarily teach? How should this work within our lives?

5. Which description of the obeyed Word do like you best? The rock, or the tree planted by the water?

Chapter Ten

Obedience is What Followers Do

My sheep listen to my voice; I know them, and they
follow me.

—JOHN 10:27

Come to me, all you who are weary and burdened, and
I will give you rest. Take my yoke upon you and learn
from me, for I am gentle and humble in heart, and you
will find rest for your souls. For my yoke is easy and my
burden is light.

—MATTHEW 11:28–30

WHAT IS THE definition of a "follower"? This is not a trick
question. A follower is, of course, one who follows someone
or something. If one follows a certain newspaper column,
it means that she reads it and that she expectantly looks
forward to seeing what each new column says. If one follows a sports team, it means that he checks out the scores,
knows who is or is not playing, and that he cares about what
happens to the team. As a follower of a certain type of management style or theory, one utilizes its practices and has
picked it out as a preferred means of leading people. Following someone or something means that one's interest is
fixed on that person or thing in such a way that the follower
is changed in some way.

So what does it mean to be a follower of Jesus? Unfortunately, we may have unknowingly changed the definition. From the above discussion, we assume that a follower of Jesus would naturally be one who allows his life to be altered by what Jesus says in Scripture and what He did as a man when He walked this earth. Obviously, as followers, we would seek out those practices that Jesus has set aside for those who pursue Him. Wouldn't we?

How have we changed that definition? It might now mean that rather than becoming followers of Jesus, we have merely "accepted Jesus as our Savior" in order to not spend an eternity in hell. I mentioned earlier that when I was a young boy, I was asked at vacation Bible school if I wanted to go to hell when I died. Since hell seemed like a pretty bad idea, I went forward and "took Jesus into my heart." Since I was now free of sin and was going to heaven, I was relieved and went on about my life. The idea of being a *follower* of Jesus was not presented to me until much later in my life. It appeared to me that there were different levels of Christianity. The regular Christians were saved and didn't go to hell, but the "good Christians" became disciples and *really* followed Jesus. I learned that the level at which one operates his spiritual life is totally his personal option. Of course, Jesus never made this distinction, but it sure got me through some wild days of high school and college with a better conscience.

Some Christians may have come to Jesus because they were told they would find a life of great joy and few problems. In fact, some may have been told that God will give them better jobs, bigger homes, and other material blessings if they simply call on the name of Jesus. After all, doesn't Jesus want to make people happy? He cannot want His followers to be weighted down by the worries of life, can He? And some Christians are told that since He will give them the desires of their heart, they should dream big. The trouble is that Jesus never promised to satisfy our every wish. The passage in Psalms actually says, "Delight yourself in the LORD and he will give you the desires of your heart" (Psalm 37:4). That verse calls on believers to first delight themselves in the Lord. As the command is obeyed, God Himself alters the actual desires of the believer. Then, the God who formed those very desires in the life of the believer will meet them. We turn it around and delight ourselves in our hopes and dreams and then rely on Jesus to make them come true.

Jesus called His disciples to give up what they had on earth in order to have a new and greater calling. While they were fishing, He said, "Come, follow me and I will make you fishers of men" (Matthew 4:19). The reaction of the disciples to this call was to leave their possessions and their families to follow Jesus. He did not offer them additional material blessings! He did not even mention a new boat or additional productivity in their fishing endeavors. In fact, he said that even foxes and birds had better homes (holes and nests) than He did (Matthew 8:20). Jesus didn't even own a home! Compared to Jesus, the foxes and birds had a better situation on the earthly scale of home ownership.

In Matthew 11:28–30, Jesus called upon His followers to

take His yoke upon them and follow Him. Oxen have yokes. The farmer puts a heavy wooden implement on his oxen and a couple of things happen. First, the oxen are fastened together, causing them to become a team. Have you ever run a two-legged race? Two runners are locked together and can only move (without falling) when they move together. The oxen, likewise, are limited in movement and can only plow a straight line when they move together. But there is another thing that happens when oxen are yoked together. They find that they have gained strength. Where one might not be able to chisel his way through tough soil and rocks, two can more easily do the job.

The deeper meaning of a "yoke" can be found in Jewish literature. It meant "the sum-total of obligations which, according to the teaching of the rabbis, a person must take upon himself."[1] The yoke of a rabbi meant the requirements that one had to fulfill in order to be a proper disciple *of that rabbi*. The yoke given to disciples by Israel's teachers was one of totally unwarranted legalism. Theirs was a system of teaching in which one's salvation depended on strict adherence to a massive set of rules and regulations.[2] The followers of this yoke were heavy-laden by its weight and unforgiving requirements. Against that background, Jesus came and announced that His rules were "easy and light." What an offer!

---

[1] William Hendriksen, *Matthew* (Baker House, Grand Rapids, Michigan, 1973), p. 504.

[2] Ibid.

How could that be true? Haven't I already stated that obedience is sometimes difficult? Now stay with me on this. Jesus calls us to be yoked to *Him*! That's why He says His yoke is easy. The burden is light because we are now connected to the greatest power source in the universe! The same Jesus who overcame death and ascended into Heaven invites us to live life with Him and to be His partner. He calls us to be yokefellows with Him in His fields. We are now coupled to Him and what we could not otherwise do, we can now accomplish because of our new Yokemate. The call of Christ is for those of us who are weary and heavy-laden by the requirements put on us by the world. It is to come and be partners with God. Even as He calls us to a new work, He promises that we will find rest because He is gentle and humble. This meek and peaceful Lord invites us to allow the weight of life to rest on His shoulders as He guides us through our lives. Who doesn't want to be in *that* relationship?

There is just one catch. Those who are yoked to Jesus will find themselves going Jesus' way and not their own way (remember, He is more powerful). Thus, the idea of obedience has a new illustration. It is a picture of being attached to God who came to earth as a man and who died for the sins of believers on the cross. Yes, He forgives His people. Yes, He saves them from an eternal life in hell (Jesus talked about hell more than anyone else in Scripture). And yes, their lives have greater joy than they ever imagined. But now they have a new plan for their lives. If one declares that he is a follower of Jesus, he finds that he must now move

God's way because he is now connected to Him.

He may take us to some frightening places, and He may challenge us to grow in new ways, yet He is in total control the whole time. My friend in Houston, Paul, uses the following illustration. Imagine that you are riding along on your motorcycle and encounter Jesus by the side of the road. Jesus says, "Let me get on . . . in fact, let me drive." He stands astride the bike and then casually turns and says, "You might want to hang on." He then pops a wheelie and fires off down the road. Together, you make hairpin turns on mountain trails. You take a jump or two. You go faster than you alone have ever gone, ride longer roads than you have ever encountered, and observe the world from heights that you would never have otherwise seen. The whole point of the ride is for you to become confident in and grow to trust your Driver. The ride is exhilarating and sometimes it even feels like you might die. When He stops, He asks, "What do you think?" You say, "Let's go again!"

So if His yoke is easy and His burden is light, why is the Christian road strewn with yokes that have yet to be taken up? In Jesus, we find One who is humble and gentle who promises that we will find rest for our souls in Him, and yet, the idea of obedience to Him continually confounds and eludes even the strongest believer. One would think that if the Creator of the Universe came to earth in order to give those whom He created an eternal mission, His creatures would be lining up to get their marching orders. What is the deal?

We have not come to grips with His true call. We think

that we have been saved in order to find earthly happiness, to make a lot of money, and to live in the best house that we can, and then when we die, Jesus will take us to be with Him in heaven (and live in an even fancier house). Instead, we have been called to a new Kingdom. We are saved in order to follow and obey Jesus Christ. Our new goal in life is to bring glory to our Creator and to help prepare the world for the day that He will return and take over. The Christian life is not about gathering all that we can get here on earth and having the most fun that we can and then go to heaven. We are called for a great purpose that may be hard (the original disciples all suffered and were killed). It may cause us to be thrown into prison (Joseph went to prison for doing the right thing—take a look at Genesis 39).

This life might cause you to actually lose your life. Check out the story of Jim Elliott in *Through the Gates of Splendor*. Elliot, true to God's call on his life, went to South America to evangelize the Auca Indians—and was murdered by them. His wife, Elisabeth, was left to suffer this loss. Her journey of obedience led her to continue his quest and to eventually lead the tribe to Christ, including the ones who actually killed her husband! The fate that awaited Jim Elliot was part of the plan to bring glory to God. As bad as it was for Elliot to be killed and to leave his family here on earth, it was the way that God chose to change those whom Jim encountered.

Still want to talk about obedience? Go back to Hebrews 11 and take a look at the stories of those who obeyed though they never saw the result of their obedience. Go read about those men and women who were killed, beheaded, and sawn in two. Their happiness on earth was adversely affected by their being yoked with Christ. I doubt seriously that they were "happy" while they were literally being cut into two pieces. Yet their eternal joy is still going on! Their burden was light because they were empowered by Jesus, who knew what it meant to suffer greatly for the cause of the Kingdom and who had come to dwell in their hearts and minds.

So, why would one want to follow this Leader who promises that the follower will be hated and persecuted on earth (John 15:18–20)? It is because it is the only way to live! The goal is not to be rich while on earth. God may grant you wealth if that is to be your role in His kingdom, but the Christian goal is to store up treasure in heaven and to be wealthy according to God's eternal scale (Matthew 6:20). How does one store up treasure in heaven? It must be to live the way that God commands. God created all people and knows what those who follow Him are supposed to do in order to fulfill their call from Him. The only way to live, then, is to be obedient to His commands. It is then, and then only, that Christians will exist for the eternity to come of which Matthew speaks in Matthew 6:20. That is real life. Paul told Timothy,

> Command those who are rich in this present world not to be arrogant nor to put their hope in wealth, which is so uncertain, but to put their hope in God, who richly provides us with everything for our enjoyment. Command them to do good, to be rich in good deeds, and to

be generous and willing to share. In this way they will lay
up treasure for themselves as a firm foundation for the
coming age, so that they may take hold of the life that is
truly life.

—1 TIMOTHY 6:17–19

And so we are conflicted. We want the greater future that
we are promised in Christ, but at the same time, we want
all the comforts in life. The very thought of losing our home
and career scares us so badly that we settle for a "half-life"
with Christ. Or so we think. In turning from a life that is
totally sold out for Jesus, we find that we have also left that
which keeps us alive. It is as Henry Scougal relates in his
ageless book, *The Life of God in the Soul of Man*:

> In a word, what our blessed Savior said of himself, is in
> some measure applicable to his followers, "that it is their
> meat and drink to do their Father's will" (John 4:34), And
> as the natural appetite is carried out toward food, though
> we should not reflect on the necessity of it for the pres-
> ervation of our lives; so are they carried with a natural
> and unforced propensity toward that which is good and
> commendable.[3]

Scougal means that we are pulled toward the will of
God as surely as we are drawn to food. But listen to this:
We are not necessarily drawn to food just because it keeps
us alive. We are attracted by the way it tastes. We love it,
and therefore, we eat. We first turn to God because we want

---

[3] Henry Scougal, *The Life of God in the Soul of Man* (Christian
Heritage, Scotland, 1996; originally published in 1677), p. 47.

the salvation that keeps us alive, but we wind up following God's will because we grow to love it. As Timothy stated above, it is how to "take hold of the life that is truly life."

In our hearts, we want to follow Christ in all that it means. We also want respect, safety, and security. But none of this is guaranteed to anyone who follows Jesus. We live in a world that believes the grass is greener on the other side of the fence. We seek that which is impossible to receive: earthly security and comfort. Interestingly enough, it *is* possible to find it eternally. All we have to do is turn our backs on what seems like the sure thing and follow a God who really is sure. We have to fight the "wisdom" of the world, which tells us that a supreme being who created the world is ridiculous. We then go after the God whose reality can be seen everywhere. Most of us spend countless hours pursuing what can be seen in order to explain away what is "unseen." Scripture tells us just the opposite, "So we fix our eyes not on what is seen, but on what is unseen. For what is seen is temporary, but what is unseen is eternal" (2 Corinthians 4:18).

We all desperately need to focus on God's unseen promises. God has given us His plan for living the life that is really life. We know that we have access to the Creator through His Son. Yet we hold onto things that only serve to drag us down. We obey the world because we can see it and touch it. We disobey God because He cannot be physically touched and His way seems like such a long haul. The shortcut is what we want, but this is exactly what flings us into sin. We are desperately in need of help. How will we find it?

Discussion Questions

1. In your neighborhood, what is the meaning of the word, "Christian"? What should the "official" definition be?

2. If there were such a thing as being a "good Christian," what would it be?

3. Is it easy or hard to imagine being yoked to Jesus? What would happen if that were so?

4. When you hear of Christians who have been martyred for their faith, what do you think?

5. How can we stop worrying about safety and start *really* pursuing God's will?

Chapter Eleven

"God, Help Me to Obey You"

People were bringing little children to Jesus to have him touch them, but the disciples rebuked them. When Jesus saw this, he was indignant. He said to them, "Let the little children come to me, and do not hinder them, for the kingdom of God belongs to such as these. I tell you the truth, anyone who will not receive the kingdom of God like a little child will never enter it." And he took the children in his arms, put his hands on them and blessed them.

As Jesus started on his way, a man ran up to him and fell on his knees before him. "Good teacher," he asked, "what must I do to inherit eternal life?"

"Why do you call me good?" Jesus answered. "No one is good—except God alone. You know the commandments: 'Do not murder, do not commit adultery, do not steal, do not give false testimony, do not defraud, honor your father and mother.'"

"Teacher," he declared, "all these I have kept since I was a boy."

Jesus looked at him and loved him. "One thing you lack," he said. "Go, sell everything you have and give to the poor, and you will have treasure in heaven. Then come, follow me."

At this the man's face fell. He went away sad, because he had great wealth. Jesus looked around and said to his disciples, "How hard it is for the rich to enter the kingdom of God!"

The disciples were amazed at his words. But Jesus said

again, "Children, how hard it is to enter the kingdom
of God! It is easier for a camel to go through the eye of
a needle than for a rich man to enter the kingdom of
God."

The disciples were even more amazed, and said to each
other, "Who then can be saved?"

Jesus looked at them and said, "With man this is
impossible, but not with God; all things are possible
with God."

Peter said to him, "We have left everything to follow
you!"

"I tell you the truth," Jesus replied, "no one who has
left home or brothers or sisters or mother or father
or children or fields for me and the gospel will fail
to receive a hundred times as much in this present
age (homes, brothers, sisters, mothers, children and
fields—and with them, persecutions) and in the age to
come, eternal life. But many who are first will be last,
and the last first."

—MARK 10:13–31

WE ALL KNOW those who seem to be skating through life.
You have seen them. Muffler waving in the wind. Hands behind their back. A big smile on their face. Eyes half closed.
This was the life of the rich man in Mark 10. On the surface,
he had it all. Yet he saw something that deeply disturbed
him. He was probably in the crowd as Jesus lifted the children up and blessed them. This man witnessed shy and
bashful children who, with a little grin, drew nearer to Jesus until He noticed them. Maybe these young ones would
inch toward Jesus, only to run away laughing as He grabbed
at them. Finally, they would end up in the arms of Jesus and
were held there securely. The rich man, with all the wealth

that one could imagine, had never seen someone like Jesus, who could debate with the smartest religious leaders in the world, yet still be attractive to children. Possibly for the first time in his life, the man realized that there was something that he did not have. He longed to be blessed by the re-markable man named Jesus.

He approached Jesus quickly; so quickly that he hit his knees and probably slid the last few steps. Forgetting that his ornate robes were dragging in the dirt, he came forward. For the moment, he did not notice that his expensive shoes had sand in them. He only wanted to get next to Jesus. I wonder if he had to nudge one of the children aside as he tried to get closer. Now he had Jesus' attention and he spoke, "Good teacher, what about me? What must I do to be saved?"

Why did the man call Jesus good? He judged everyone relatively. Jesus must be good. Look how the children adored Him. The man had probably heard of Jesus' miracles. Any-one who did things like that had to be good. Jesus' question to the man—"Why do you call me good?"—was aimed at showing him that only God was truly good and a man without God could not be good. Of course, Jesus *was* good. He was God on earth and, therefore, was perfect. The man could not have known that at this moment, however. Jesus' suggestion of obeying the commandments focused on the man's major issue. He thought that being good emanated from what one did. Inaccurately, he told Jesus that he had obeyed the commandments since he was a boy. The man must have hoped that this would have made him good.

Jesus looked at the man and loved him. That short statement describes the heart of Jesus. Though this man was so wrong about his life, Jesus saw him in love and knew what he could be. Then, in order to uncover the sin in his life, Jesus made a disturbing statement. He told him to go sell all that he had and give the money to the poor. If the man thought that his actions could save him, Jesus was throwing down the gauntlet. Jesus asked him to give up all of his possessions. That's what he could *do*! If the man thought that he could get to God by doing, then Jesus gave him a whopper "to do." If he could do that, he would gain God's acceptance and would have the treasure in heaven that his heart truly sought. He had come to Jesus seeking something that he did not have—real love. *That* was what he wanted. But now a strange thing happened. The man hung his head and left. He could not do what Jesus asked. He loved his possessions too much.

Why did he leave sad? Scripture says that he was sad because he was wealthy. What? All of us would like to be wealthy. Most of us dream about a rich uncle from Idaho who leaves us ten million dollars as our inheritance from the potato farm. How could someone be sad *because* he had great wealth? Because his trust in earthly riches kept him from his heart's desire. Money separated him from Jesus, not because it was evil, but because he loved it more than what he really wanted, the love of God. And because of that, the man walked away, presumably to a life of misery.

The rich man only missed one step in his journey to God. He did not ask Jesus for help in obeying the command that he was given. The man by himself could never have sold all of his possessions and given the money to the poor. And neither could we! Jesus could have empowered him to obey the difficult command that He laid out. The rich man needed only to ask for help and he would have had it. But he really didn't want it. He did not want to obey badly enough to seek the empowerment that Jesus alone could give. And he went away sad to live his life apart from the Creator that designed him. God had tucked away many hidden gifts and talents within him that could only be revealed by Jesus. To live without Christ was indeed a sad prospect.

The disciples could not believe it when they heard Jesus relate how hard it is for a rich man to enter the kingdom of heaven. It was so hard that a camel could go through the eye of a needle easier than for a rich man to enter heaven! (And no, Jesus was not talking about a real camel that could kneel down and squeeze through some obscure gate in the Jerusalem wall called "The Eye of the Needle." That gate never existed and that attempt to change Jesus' illustration only stands to negate the power of Christ.) Jesus was purposely giving an impossible example. It would be unattainable for a rich man to do enough good deeds in order to enter God's kingdom. It would only be possible with the empowerment of Jesus. The disciples asked Jesus, "Who then can be saved?" We would *all* have trouble selling our possessions and giving the money to the poor. We all hang on to what we can see. How can anyone be saved?

In answer to his own unachievable example, Jesus told them that God could do anything, even that which seems impossible. In one of the more poignant moments of Scripture, Peter stepped up. Maybe he looked down the road at the retreating rich man, then to his friends, and then to Jesus. "We have left everything to follow you." Peter was telling Jesus, "We have nothing left. We are banking on You, Jesus. What will happen to *us*?" Maybe Peter had just realized that they had truly given up everything to follow Jesus. The cost may have seemed extremely high at that moment.

Jesus reassured the disciples by telling them that their sacrifice would not be in vain. No one who left family or goods or real estate would be disappointed. They would receive a hundred times more than they left, both in this world and in the world to come. And they would also receive persecutions. This encouragement—yes, even with the warning about persecution—was intended to strengthen them. God would take care of them, in their present life and in the life to come.

There was one more warning. All of those who try to be first in this world will find out soon enough that they are really last. The rich man would finish life behind the disciples. The poor on this earth would become rich in things to come. Without Jesus, the rich in this world will be lost in eternity. Can you imagine that? Pick out the richest, most influential person that you have ever known. Without Jesus, he or she will miss everything that is lasting and eternal. As important as they are on this earth, unless they meet the Savior, these people will be unimportant in eternity. Dead last. The love that is sought by all, will evade even those who look like they have everything. In the end, they will have nothing unless they know the saving grace of Jesus Christ.

This story is a reminder to those who do not possess a relationship with Jesus Christ. They are more than poor; they are bankrupt without His unfailing love. They have no ability, in and of themselves, to earn or buy the love of God. That love is offered to each of us in the death and resurrection of Jesus. All of us, like the rich man, seek the love that only Jesus can give. And without a relationship with Jesus, we will never find it.

Once we have been forgiven and have joined Christ in an eternal relationship, how can we really be men and women who follow Him despite the cost? Jesus said:

> Ask and it will be given to you; seek and you will find; knock and the door will be opened to you. For everyone who asks receives; he who seeks finds; and to him who knocks, the door will be opened.
>
> Which of you, if his son asks for bread, will give him a stone? Or if he asks for a fish, will give him a snake? If you, then, though you are evil, know how to give good gifts to your children, how much more will your Father in heaven give good gifts to those who ask him!
>
> —MATTHEW 7:7–11

Ask God to help you to obey Him. If our knowledge and love of God will knit our hearts to His and our obedience will cause us to remain in Him, we should be asking for His help everyday. How could we not? And isn't that the kind of prayer that God would have us pray? Can you imagine praying the prayer, "God, please help me to obey You," only to hear God say, "No"? Of course not! God would embrace a prayer like that. We have His promise if we will seek Him, we will find Him. The prayer for help in our obedience is what it means to seek God. If we knock, the Lord will open the door. The service to Him, that only He can empower, will indeed open wide the pathway to Him. We are not saved by our obedience, but we understand more about Jesus when we do His work. We come to know Jesus as we obey Him.

If I asked my boys to sweep out the garage and later one of them came to me and said, "Dad, we have a problem in the garage and we need your help in finishing the job that you gave us," what kind of dad would I be if I did not help? If my boys were trying to carry out my wishes, I would walk out with them and help them do the task. I would be happy that they came to me with the problem. Our perfect God will help us obey Him. He will. He has given us a set of marching orders that will allow us to participate in establishing His kingdom. When we seek Him, He tells us that we will find Him. When we knock on His door, He promises to answer. So if we ask Him to help us obey Him, won't He be available? Our Father, who knows how to give good gifts, can be trusted as we attempt to live out the life that He has given to us.

So why don't you stop right now and ask for His help? What is keeping you from doing that? Is it because you don't know what He will do with your life? Or is it because you really love this world and you are afraid that what you get in return might not be as good as you could get for yourself? What a mistake it would be to fear to obey God because we do not believe that He will give us good things. A God who is great enough to create the world can also give each of His people exactly what they need in order to live. The above passage from Matthew 7 says that He loves His children and will give them what they need. The children should then be confident enough to ask for His power to do what He wants them to do.

So get with it. Start your day, everyday, by asking God for the desire and the ability to obey Him. Search the Bible to find those commands and see what God will do as you attempt to carry out His wishes. You won't be disappointed.

"God, help me to obey You."

Discussion Questions

1. What are several reasons why the young man in Mark 10 might have been attracted to Jesus?

2. Why do you think the young man in Mark 10 walked away sad? How can you relate to his sadness?

3. Why did Jesus give the illustration of the camel going through the eye of a needle? Why give an impossible example?

4. How could Matthew 7:7–11 change your prayer life?

5. How do you envision God? Do you think of Him as a loving God, or One who is frequently impatient and mad at us? What causes you to think as you do?

Chapter Twelve

The Result of Obeying God

"I am the true vine, and my Father is the gardener. He cuts off every branch in me that bears no fruit, while every branch that does bear fruit he prunes so that it will be even more fruitful. You are already clean because of the word I have spoken to you. Remain in me, and I will remain in you. No branch can bear fruit by itself; it must remain in the vine. Neither can you bear fruit unless you remain in me.

"I am the vine; you are the branches. If a man remains in me and I in him, he will bear much fruit; apart from me you can do nothing. If anyone does not remain in me, he is like a branch that is thrown away and withers; such branches are picked up, thrown into the fire and burned. If you remain in me and my words remain in you, ask whatever you wish, and it will be given you. This is to my Father's glory, that you bear much fruit, showing yourselves to be my disciples.

"As the Father has loved me, so have I loved you. Now remain in my love. If you obey my commands, you will remain in my love, just as I have obeyed my Father's commands and remain in his love. I have told you this so that my joy may be in you and that your joy may be complete. My command is this: Love each other as I have loved you. Greater love has no one than this, that he lay down his life for his friends. You are my friends if you do what I command. I no longer call you servants, because a servant does not know his master's business. Instead, I have called you friends, for everything that I learned from my Father I have made known to you. You

> did not choose me, but I chose you and appointed you
> to go and bear fruit—fruit that will last. Then the Father
> will give you whatever you ask in my name. This is my
> command: Love each other."
>
> —JOHN 15:1–17

OK, THAT WAS your second chance to pray a prayer that would change your life. Did you do it? If not, please go back and re-read chapter 11. If you want your life to be changed, you should want to pray life-changing prayers. What could more affect your life than to pray that God would first help you love Him, and secondly, that He would help you to obey Him? I guarantee you that you will never be the same.

What will happen if you pray those prayers? What kinds of changes might you start noticing in your life? In John 15, Jesus mentions the idea of "remaining in Him." That, according to Jesus, is a result from obeying Him. Perhaps it would be a good time to review what "remaining in Him" is.

One of the great doctrines of Scripture is "union with Christ." The Creator of the Universe has come to dwell in our lives. We are one with Him. The very hope of glory is "Christ in you" (Colossians 1:27). Paul also stated in Colossians 2:9–10, that we have been given the "fullness of Christ" in a similar way that the fullness of God the Father dwelt in Christ. All of the characteristics of God are fully alive in Christ, and we have been given that same fullness in Christ. Think about it. God came to earth as the perfect man Jesus who forgives our sins, and then He comes in the form of the Holy Spirit to live in us.

As I recounted earlier, when I was a child I was asked to come forward in my church and "ask Jesus into my heart." I could never figure that one out. How could Jesus get into my heart? It seemed to me that it would be quite uncomfortable for both of us. Now, as an adult, I know more about how it works. Jesus implants in me His Spirit, who causes me to obey Him. I become "one with Christ" and now I want to be like Him. My desire to obey does not come from me. It is given to me through the work of Christ and the Holy Spirit so that my life reflects the life of Christ. Because of my sin, this reflection is not perfect, but as I grow with Christ, it gets better. I am able to obey in greater ways than before. The motivation to do God's will is a gift from God. He shows me in Scripture what I should do and then helps me to do it.

So what can I expect as a result of my prayer of obedience? From John 15, we will take note of four changes. Each will be a result of our union with Christ. My obedience knits me to the life of Christ. The story of the vine tells us that we are His branches that have been grafted into the vine, which is Christ. The gardener, the Father, carefully tends the vineyard in order to maximize its output. He prunes bad branches so that precious nutrients can come to the good branches.

Jesus began this discourse as He led the disciples out of the upper room, down through the Kidron Valley, and back up toward the Garden of Gethsemane. As they walked they would have found themselves among the vineyards that grew there. Jesus, as He did many times, used His

surroundings to illustrate His points. Jesus may have pointed to the vines as He told the apostles that He was the vine
and they were the branches. He challenged them to remain
in Him, which would be a result of obeying Him, which He
directly stated in verse 10.

Result #1: You will produce fruit

The first result of our prayer for obedience is found in
verse 5. Jesus promised that if His disciples remained in
Him, they would produce much fruit. If they remained
apart from Him, they would produce nothing. The fruit
that they would bear might come in two forms. First, the
fruit is Christ-likeness. Galatians 5:22 details the "fruit of
the Spirit," which are the very characteristics of Jesus: "love,
joy, peace, patience, kindness, goodness, faithfulness, gen-
tleness and self-control." As we follow and obey Christ, He
will lead us into circumstances that will cause our lives to be
conformed to His image (Romans 8:28–29). We will see the
characteristics of Jesus' life begin to be displayed in ours.

The other fruits of our life are the people whose faith
is grown due to the presence of Jesus in us. As our new life
becomes evident, others are won over to the faith through
us. They are the fruit that is produced by God. We cannot
take the credit, but God uses us to impact those He chooses
to touch.

The old saying that "the apple doesn't fall far from the
tree" refers mainly to our children, who grow up and behave just like their parents did. The apple falls; it produces

a seed, which then grows another tree just like it.

This statement might be of use in describing our faith. The fruit that grows from us serves as seed for others around us who grab onto the life with Christ. That is because the fruit in us actually came from Jesus who perfectly displayed those characteristics listed in Galatians 5:22.

Result #2: You will pray as Jesus would

The second result is that as we remain in Christ, through obedience, we will pray as Jesus would. John 15:7 says, "If you remain in me and my words remain in you, ask whatever you wish, and it will be given to you." If we are in Christ and are obedient to Him, our desires will begin to be like His. The reason that we can ask for whatever we wish is because He will lead us to pray those prayers. His desires become our desires. We can now be bold in our conversations with Him since He is the motivation for our requests. We will be led by Him to pray like Him. Now remember, we will never be perfect in this, but as we mature in our relationship with Christ, we will become more like Him.

Paul told the Romans:

> In the same way, the Spirit helps us in our weakness. We do not know what we ought to pray for, but the Spirit himself intercedes for us with groans that words cannot express. And he who searches our hearts knows the mind of the Spirit, because the Spirit intercedes for the saints in accordance with God's will.
>
> —ROMANS 8:26–27

We pray as Jesus prayed when He was on the earth:

> During the days of Jesus' life on earth, he offered up
> prayers and petitions with loud cries and tears to the one
> who could save him from death, and he was heard be-
> cause of his reverent submission.
>
> —HEBREWS 5:7

We, also, will be led to pray by the Holy Spirit whom we possess in our being. The Spirit directs our interests to be in line with those of God and therefore our prayers will reflect the heart of God. These prayers are answered as John 15:7 reflects because they come directly from the Spirit of God.

Result #3: You will remain in His love

Third, as we are obedient to Christ, we will remain in His love. We are like the tree in Psalm 1 that is planted by the water. Such a tree sinks its roots down deep and becomes practically immovable. In fact, Jesus makes an unbelievable comparison. He says in John 15:10 that, just as He has obeyed His Father's commands and now remains in His love, so we will experience that same union with Him. We will remain in Jesus' love in the same way that He remains in the Father's love! Some may argue that this is impossible, but Jesus said it right here in John 15. He told us this so that our joy might be complete. And what joy that would be! To experience the love of Jesus like He experiences the Father's love would be a great delight. No wonder that He said that His joy would be in us.

Many have struggled with the idea of joy. In today's world, it seems that joy is a distant dream. Isn't that amazing? In our modern world, we have more of everything. We have technology that can do fantastic things. Diseases that killed people only fifty years ago have now been wiped out. Life expectancy continues to be extended. We can communicate with one another at anytime from all over the world. The news events of each day are available to us twenty-four hours a day. The wind can generate electricity for us and, lo and behold, we can even power our cars with corn!

There is only one thing we are missing. We are not becoming more joyous. During the fifties, we dreamed of a thirty-hour workweek. We imagined a future in which robots did all of our work. Instead, we have found that each technological advancement brings on new stress. Now we have email that puts us in touch all the time and what happens? People are never off work! They receive messages from their companies around the clock. There is nowhere to hide and now they work all the time. While we love our phones and computers, they also bring us a great deal of anxiety. Our companies expect us to be available continuously. We have wrecks in our cars because we cannot stay off our cell phones for five minutes. Laws have to be made that make it illegal to text each other as we drive down the highway at seventy miles per hour.

We desperately need and desire the joy that Jesus promises, yet we are afraid of the obedience that will bring it to us. There is no doubt that God planned for us to enjoy rest after we worked. That was His model on the seventh day after He created the universe. He rested. There is now very little rest for us, and there is very little time to consider how

God would like to change the world through us. It is a gigantic circle of chaos in which we find ourselves. We need prayer. We need the desire to ask God to make us obedient to Him. There is no greater rest than is found in a life that is obedient to the One who created us. In living a life that resonates with Him, we will find the true blessing of life.

Result #4: We Become Friends of Jesus

Finally, as obedient men and women, we become friends of Jesus:

> You are my friends if you do what I command. I no longer call you servants, because a servant does not know his master's business. Instead, I have called you friends, for everything that I learned from my Father I have made known to you.
>
> —JOHN 15:14–15

Jesus cannot be saying that it is through our obedience that we achieve a relationship with Him. We know clearly that our knowledge and relationship with God comes only from God as our gift through faith (Ephesians 2:8–9). What, then, can this friendship be? Jesus goes on to explain. If we are mere servants, we would not know the purposes of Jesus' kingdom. We would just do what we are told. However, as heirs of the Kingdom (Romans 8:17), we actually participate in the work of Jesus. We know what we are to do through the Word and by doing it we are allowed to be called friends of Jesus. What an honor!

Everyone wants to know the rich and famous. If we meet someone who is well known in the world, we want to tell everyone we know. I know a few people who are in the public eye. I find myself bringing those relationships into my conversations so that others will be impressed with my sphere of acquaintances. *I* must be important since I know someone who *is* important. We press to shake the hands of those we consider significant. These people are photographed and asked to sign scraps of paper in order that we would remember their presence with us.

One summer we were in the nation's capital and we attended the Friday night parade at the Marine Barracks Washington, the country's oldest Marine post. The same night that we were there, the president was also in attendance. To see the president of the United States arrive is something to behold. Traffic was halted. Pedestrians were stopped on the sidewalks and those in restaurants were not allowed to exit. The motorcade carrying the president had five or six cars and vans with armed guards visible. Numerous motorcycle police rode in front and behind the motorcade. And the Wernettes were right there! We must really be important. Of course, we told everyone we knew that we had been very close when POTUS arrived. (POTUS means "President of the United States." If you had seen the president, you would know that.) We were thrilled to participate in the arrival of such a significant figure.

So we all desire to know and be known by those who are important. Now we are given the chance to be friends with the Creator of the world. How would you like to know what the president knows? Just think how neat it would be to know all the codes, to know how to call up the British Prime

Minister, and to live in that big house. But forget about all that; Jesus says that we can know what *He* knows! We may not be able to be friends with the president, but we can be friends with the One who created the president. As Jesus' friends, He will enlighten us and tell us everything that the Father had taught Him. That is amazing.

My obedience also shows me the sufficiency of God. Sometimes we get way out on a limb in what we try to do in the Kingdom. It is then that God steps in and shows us what He can do through our small, human efforts. The feeding of the five thousand in Mark 6 was as much for the disciples as it was for those who were hungry. The result was that the apostles saw, through their obedience, what Jesus could accomplish through them. The sending of the seventy-two (Luke 10) gave Jesus great joy as these disciples came back and reported their successes, which He had done through them. The miraculous catch of fish in Luke 5 illustrated to the disciples that their failure could become success as they obediently followed the command of Jesus "to throw the nets on the other side of the boat." Peter was brought to the realization of the power and perfection of Jesus and of his own sin and inadequacy.

I am reminded, through my obedience, that Jesus lives in me. In John 15:5, He says, "apart from me, you can do nothing." It is His presence in me that causes me to obey Him. His life in me can be seen through my obedience. It reminds me that He is there. And therefore, it causes me to want to be closer to Him. It causes me to remain in Him. When I see the behavior of Christ in me, I am drawn closer to Jesus. My obedience, implanted in me by Christ, keeps me in Christ. I want to know more as I experience His like-ness. I obey through faith and when I see His fruits in me, I am now surer of my life in Him.

The experiences of faith keep me coming back. When I eat a great piece of fruit, I am drawn back for more. In the summer, my family loves peaches. When my wife, Suzie, brings home some really good ones, we ask her to get more when she is back at the store. As I experience God's fruit through my obedience and His blessing, I am drawn back for more. My obedience may produce fruit that I can see as a result of God's enablement. I want more. I want to see more of God because my obedience allows me to experience Him.

Real peace can only be known through the One who created this world. The God of the Universe came to earth in order to invite us to join Him in a great mission. Our new job is now to point the world to the glory of God. This task that He has bestowed upon us becomes real as we begin to venture down the path of obedience. The prayer, "God, help me to obey You," is the key that will unlock the door to your vision of His kingdom. Will He answer you? He absolutely will. We close this discussion with the verse that reminds us that God is willing to do more than we ever imagined. We should all ask God to change us to be people who want to complete the instructions that He has for us.

> Now to Him who is able to do far more abundantly be-yond all that we ask or think, according to the power that works within us, to Him be the glory in the church and in Christ Jesus to all generations forever and ever. Amen.
>
> —EPHESIANS 3:20

Discussion Questions

1. Why do we constantly need to remember Colossians 1:27, "Christ in you, the hope of glory"?

2. If we really believed Colossians 2:9–10 (that we have the fullness of Christ dwelling in us), what would that lead us to attempt?

3. Of the results of our prayer for obedience that are listed in this chapter, what one do you believe in most strongly?

4. Why don't people in our world experience more joy? What message should we as Christians bring to those who say there is no joy in their life?

5. Can real peace be found apart from Christ? What about those folks that seem happy without Him?

6. What does Ephesians 3:20 imply for your life? Do you believe it? What are you not praying about that you should?

Chapter Thirteen

Teach Others to Love and Obey God

> Then the eleven disciples went to Galilee, to the mountain where Jesus had told them to go. When they saw him, they worshiped him; but some doubted. Then Jesus came to them and said, "All authority in heaven and on earth has been given to me. Therefore go and make disciples of all nations, baptizing them in the name of the Father and of the Son and of the Holy Spirit, and teaching them to obey everything I have commanded you. And surely I am with you always, to the very end of the age."
>
> —MATTHEW 28:16–20

WE HAVE DISCUSSED two great priorities of the Christian faith—to love and obey God. Wholeheartedness is found in these two commands. The command to love God with all of our being is quite clear. Jesus said it on numerous occasions. When we boil our lives down to the essentials, there is nothing that we can do that is more important than loving God. Jesus said it, and we should believe it and pursue it. The second concept stems from loving God. It is to obey God. If obedience proves our love for God, we should want to do nothing less than obey. If we want to remain in Him, there is no alternative than that of obeying our Father. What Christian would not want to be deeply connected to the Creator? Jesus said the way to that closeness is through obedience. These two commands should become our passion. We should pray that nothing would interrupt our ability to love and obey God.

A disciple of Jesus must be totally committed to what Jesus says. When one is confronted with Jesus' sacrifice on the cross, he either loves or rejects Him. There is no middle ground. When Jesus is loved, the follower is compelled by that love (2 Corinthians 5:14) to become the person that God created him or her to be. The love for God results in nothing less than a desire to obey Him. As that love grows, the desire to obey God will also grow. Our hope should be that we will become wholehearted followers of Jesus. The Psalmist said it like this:

> May your unfailing love come to me, O LORD,
>   your salvation according to your promise;
> Then I will answer the one who taunts me,
>   for I trust in your word.
> Do not snatch the word of truth from my mouth,
>   for I have put my hope in your laws.
> I will always obey your law,
>   for ever and ever.
>
> —PSALM 119:41–44

The love of God causes the Christian to obey. As was described earlier, the ardent follower of God seeks to comply with God's instruction in the Word. The Holy Spirit empowers the believer to do it. If faith is borne out in obedience, then as one prays for more faith, the prayer will be most likely followed by the opportunity to obey. As evident in Psalm 119, the lover of God is one who actively pursues Scripture in an attempt to obey it.

A good place to start this process is by obeying those commands that are most obvious and uppermost in the mind of Christ. One would want to begin with following the most important directives that Jesus gave. This is not to say that *all* are not important. Certainly, they are. It does stand to reason, however, that Jesus may have given certain commands to His followers that were constantly uppermost in His mind. In fact, I am now going to ask you to find the "greatest" of His instructions and then challenge you to obey it.

How would one know which of His commands were most important? Whether it is a speech, a lesson, a book, or a song, major points are usually made toward the end of a work. The reason for that is simple. What is said last is easily remembered. A speaker generally saves his best idea for the conclusion. People will keep that in mind since it was the last thing that they heard. Is it possible to find a command of Jesus that would encompass His way of living that He would want His followers to exhibit?

When our kids were young, we had to have a babysitter when Suzie and I went out for the evening. The babysitter would arrive and we would give all of the instructions. It really became fun when our two kids were about nine and twelve. I would tell them, in front of the babysitter, to make sure that they went to bed on time and also to absolutely not duct tape yet another babysitter to the tree in the backyard. The sitter was *pretty sure* I was kidding. Usually,

I gave the important instructions just before we left. On most nights, I would lean back in the door and give my last orders. It was these instructions that were most important. I would look at my boys, at the babysitter, and then back to the boys, saying something like, "Oh yeah, don't eat too much candy," or "Make sure that you pick up your toys," or "Above all, go to bed on time." My last words were my most critical directions and expressed my concerns. I was counting on Ryan and Chris to obey my last request.

Jesus spent three years with His apostles. During that time, He taught them many things. Through good times and difficult times, He gave them His instructions. Then came the day when it was time for Him to go back to His Father. He was ready to leave His friends, and He gave them His most strategic command. He was handing over His life's ministry to them. He was leaving eleven men with whom He had spent His entire ministry. They were now prepared for the task that He was going to give them. Just before He left, He "leaned back in" and gave them His final instructions.

Matthew 28:19–20 records these words. The actual commands of Jesus are preceded with some foundational thoughts. Matthew 28:17 says, "When they saw him, they worshiped him; but some doubted." It is beneficial to note that two things happened here. First, Jesus was worshipped as the risen Lord. He had appeared several times to them and they now saw that He had come back from the dead and He was worthy of their worship. There was little question in the minds of most of them as to who Jesus was and what He had accomplished. Second, the passage indicates that some doubted. Did they doubt that Jesus was resurrected? Or were they not sure that the man in front of them was indeed Jesus? Or maybe they doubted their mission with Jesus. Whatever those doubts were, Jesus seemed to address them in His commands that followed. After He spoke, there were no doubts whatsoever as to the nature of their mission. That was made very clear.

Jesus began by stating that all authority in heaven and on earth had been given to Him. He was now in possession of God's influence over all creation. In Colossians 1:18, Paul said, ". . . that in everything he [Jesus] might have the supremacy." If Jesus were now capable of running the entire universe, what would He tell the disciples? How would they react to this authority? This was the One who would direct the whole of God's creation. If the president of a large company or the president of the United States gave an order, those under his authority would want to obey. The disciples of Jesus listened as He gave them His final instructions.

As Jesus left the earth, He commanded them to make disciples of people in all nations and people groups. There are several verbs in the statement, but for now, focus on "make disciples" as the main verb. The word for *disciple* means a follower or a learner.[1] Jesus was asking His disciples to go make disciples of their own. He wanted them to help men and women of the entire world to become learners and

---

[1]   For a discussion of this, see Myron S. Augsburger, *The Communicator's Commentary: Matthew* (Word Publishing, Waco, Texas, 1982), p. 330.

followers of His ways and teachings. Notice that He did not say, "Go make converts." This was not a call to lead people to merely make decisions for Christ. In today's world, that has become the goal for many churches and ministries. Certainly, that is important because it is the first step to discipleship, but it was not what Jesus told His disciples that day. He said He wanted them to make disciples. In his commentary on Matthew, evangelical scholar William Hendriksen said this:

> Mere mental understanding does not as yet make a disciple. It is part of the picture, in fact an important part, but only a part. The truth learned must be practiced. It must be appropriated by heart, mind, and will, so that one remains or abides in the truth. Only then is one truly Christ's "disciple" (John 8:31).[2]

Jesus asked them to baptize their disciples in the name of the Father, the Son, and the Holy Spirit. He also directed the apostles to teach them to obey everything that He had commanded. As men and women are brought into God's kingdom, the act of teaching them to obey the commands of God is extremely important. In baptism, one is sealed and marked as belonging to the family of God. What must happen after one is baptized? He is taught the fundamentals of the faith. It is the responsibility of the church to continue the education of the one who is baptized. The key is that Jesus commanded His disciples to teach their disciples

---

[2] Hendriksen, pp. 999–1000.

to obey. Disciples are made through obedience. To summarize the quote from Hendriksen above, a disciple is only a disciple because of his following Jesus through his obedience. Look at it this way: One is baptized because he has come to love Jesus, and then he is taught to follow Jesus through obedience.

Finally, Jesus said that He would be with them until the "end of the age" or, as most would interpret it, until the end of time. What a comfort for these men at such a disturbing time! Their Teacher was leaving them. Who would take His place? How would they survive? They would be able to complete the task that He was giving them only because of His presence with them. Maybe they remembered the words of Jesus on the night of His betrayal, "I will not leave you as orphans; I will come to you. Before long, the world will not see me anymore, but you will see me. Because I live, you also will live" (John 14:18–19). He not only left them with a great task, but with a Great Presence. They would be able to obey because He was with them through the Holy Spirit.

If you had been there, would there have been a question as to what Jesus wanted you to do? Is there any doubt in your mind that Jesus wants each of us to make disciples? He gave us His most important directive on the day in which He ascended to heaven. He intended to communicate that, as we go along in our lives, we are to make disciples. This command is not complicated or mysterious. He said what He meant. We are to make disciples. Does anyone out there disagree? How could you? It was His last word to us. And, as Dr. Howard Hendricks has said, "Last words are lasting words."

The problem is that we think we don't know exactly what it means to make disciples. We are not sure how to do it. Here are some of our questions regarding disciple making:

- What information should I give disciples? What do I teach them?

- Is there a certain curriculum that will produce disciples?

- Does teaching Sunday school constitute discipleship?

- Is preaching a sermon the same as disciple making?

- How do I find potential disciples?

- Isn't making disciples counter-productive to building bigger churches?

The list goes on and on. Seemingly, we are befuddled by this command to disciple. Even as we worked on this book, one of my editors mentioned that I had left out the most obvious question above. The first question, he said, was to ask "who" I was to disciple. I agreed that I had not asked "who?" but then I told him that he had it wrong. The big question is, *Will I obey Jesus in this most important command?* Once I decide to obey the last command of Jesus, the "who" is a secondary matter. The real issue is a question of obedience. After that decision is made, the "who" is almost insignificant. Later in this book, we will discuss how we find our disciple, but for now we must decide if we will even look.

The last command that Jesus gave us was to make disciples, and therefore, that should be our goal. And if His greatest commandment was to love God, shouldn't that be what we teach others? Since His desire was also for each of us to obey Him, that is what we should instruct others to do. It is really a simple task. Here it is: *Go find people and teach them to love and obey God*. That is what Jesus did with the disciples. He taught them to love the Father and to obey the Father.

How did He do it? He used many teaching techniques. He let them follow Him around. He had discussions with them. I'll bet that He asked and answered a lot of questions. Sometimes, He told them things right out, like "If you want to be great, you have to be a servant," and "If you want to be first, be last." The disciples asked Jesus how often they should forgive each other, suggesting that seven times seemed like a lot of forgiveness. Jesus said to forgive seventy times seven (Matthew 18:22), which represented a virtually unlimited number. That would indeed be a task. Jesus also said that if someone slaps you in the face; offer them your other cheek. He was teaching them how to love others as He would. We can help our disciples to love God by showing them how Scripture calls us to love God.

Jesus not only taught them with words, He modeled how to live and love God. One day the apostles asked Him to teach them to pray. Ever wonder why they asked that? It was most likely because every time they went looking for Him, He was praying. Finally, late in His ministry, they asked Him, "Lord, teach us to pray." They wanted to do what their Leader did. He also modeled servanthood when the authorities insulted Him on the night of His betrayal.

Though His captors ridiculed him, He never lashed back as we might do. He displayed His character by not answering insult for insult (1 Peter 2:23). We also must teach our disciples by modeling. They should see us worship and pray. They watch as we react to events in our lives, some of which are difficult and maybe, insulting. Hopefully, they can observe our behavior and know that it comes from our relationship with Jesus.

There were other times when Jesus made His apostles think. He said that when a farmer plants a seed, the kind of soil on which it lands would determine how it grows (Mark 4). Sometimes, it landed on rocky soil and would not grow. At other times, it would fall on good soil and produce a huge result. Why didn't He just say that His disciples would plant God's Word and sometimes those who heard it would reject it? Maybe Jesus wanted them to puzzle over His words. He wanted them to think it through and realize that being a part of His kingdom would be difficult. It would be hard work to spread God's Word. In order to grow, disciples must be made to think. We have to ask questions. One of the great modes of learning is the discovery method. When students have to mull truth over, they figure it out and learn it well.

Lead your students to wonder what it would be like to live as Mark 4 suggests. Teach them to love God so much that they are willing to throw out the love of God to everyone they can. Help them to accept the crop that God gives. What if we could raise disciples like that? That is exactly what we are supposed to do. Such a life would require obedience. Jesus tells us to put out the Word. Do not hide your light under a bushel, but allow the world to observe it in your behavior. Go ahead; put it out there, because Jesus said that we should. Allow Him to decide the results, no matter what they look like to us.

Do you yourself want to live out Mark 4? If you would, then maybe it is time for a change. The prayer to love God will lead you to make disciples. True love for Him will lead us to want to obey Him even if our efforts to do so seem fruitless to us. The greatest disciplers—like Paul for, instance—had many failures. Paul threw out truth in a little place called Lystra (Acts 14). They were so "excited" to hear the Word that they stoned Paul and drug him out of town thinking that he was dead. Gee, isn't disciple making fun? Paul also lost disciples. As he closed the book of Second Timothy, he mentioned that Demas—"because he loved the world"—had deserted him (2 Timothy 4:10). Imagine how much time Paul spent with Demas. From a worldly perspective, Paul failed with Demas and at Lystra, but it was obedience in action. Two thousand years later, the work of God through Paul *still goes on* because of his faithfulness to the command of Jesus, to "make disciples."

I hope that your love for God leads you to obey Him so intensely that you, too, are willing to live a life of disappointment and heartache if that is what God asks you to do. The following chapters will continue this discussion of disciple making. Just remember: the main goal is to teach those around us to love and obey God. I guarantee you that you can do it—if you want to love and obey Him also.

Discussion Questions

1. Discuss the proposition that the heart of discipleship is found in loving and obeying God. Is there anything within discipleship that is not found in these two?

2. Can we follow Jesus with less than a wholehearted commitment? Why do some try?

3. Why do you think the "some" doubted in Matthew 28:17? Can you identify with their doubt?

4. Contrast "making converts" with "making disciples." If someone is especially gifted at evangelism, what should they do for those whom they lead to Christ?

5. Jesus said that all authority in heaven and earth had been given to Him. How does this enhance His command to make disciples?

6. What keeps you from making disciples? What do you think would happen if you asked God to help you overcome this issue?

Chapter Fourteen

As You Go

Therefore go and make disciples of all nations.
—MATTHEW 28:19

WE HAVE BEEN discussing the phrase above from Matthew 28 and now it's time to make sure that we know what it really implies. This is important because some of you might be thinking that you cannot make disciples because you do not want to go to Africa or to the inner cities of Chicago or New York. There is a possibility that you have misunderstood this phrase. You may be closer to making disciples than you think. Before you rush out and "go," let's take a look at what "go" really means and its implications for you.

Matthew 28:19 reads in most English translations, "Go and make disciples." The casual reader would obviously believe the main verb is "go" and the second is "make." Some people then say, "I can't go. I am raising a family. I am the owner of a company. I cannot quit my responsibilities in order to go somewhere and get involved in some ministry." So they do not make disciples. They just keep living and keep disobeying Jesus because they do not think they can *go*. But that may not be what Jesus had in mind when He made His statement.

The word "go" in this sentence is actually not a verb. It is a participle. Please don't think that I am a language expert.

I actually had to look up "participle" on the internet. For those who need a refresher course in high school English, a participle is a verb that serves much like an adjective that describes a noun (with apologies to any English majors for my brief definition). An example would be, "she had a smiling face." The word "smiling" functions to describe her face. The verb in that sentence is "had."

A literal Greek translation of Matthew 28:19 might read, "Going therefore disciple you all nations."[1] William Hendriksen, in his commentary on Matthew, says this:

> Literally the original says, "Having gone, therefore, make disciples . . ." In such cases the participle as well as the verb that follows it can be—in the present case must be—interpreted as having imperative force. "Make disciples" is by itself an imperative. It is a brisk command, an order.[2]

The phrase could then be translated, "as you go" or "in your goings" or "having gone," make disciples. The "going" was assumed. Why be so precise over this phrase? It is important because many have misinterpreted the statement in the past and in doing so, have misinformed others as to the actual command that was given.

What is the implication of the statement if it read, "As you go, make disciples"? It would mean that as you go along

---

[1] *The Zondervan Parallel New Testament in Greek and English* (Zondervan, Grand Rapids, Michigan, 1975), p. 101.

[2] Hendriksen, p. 999.

in your life, you are to obey Jesus by making disciples. As you raise your kids, make disciples. Teach your kids to love and obey Jesus. As you own your company and try to make money, make disciples of your employees—and even your clients! If you work for someone else, make disciples of fellow employees and maybe even your boss. Be careful with this, of course. You cannot ignore your job responsibilities and go walking around the job just sharing your faith. You would get fired. However, you can do your work with such passion and completeness that it will point others to the faith. Do not shy away from verbally sharing your faith at work if the occasion comes up. You may get a chance to share your faith in *words* because of your *actions*. One of your "goings" is your job.

If this is a correct translation, and all the experts say it is, the command to make disciples is not that complicated. You need only to take note of where you are, and then make disciples of those who are there with you.

I love the stories of Chick-fil-A and Hobby Lobby. These two companies have decided that since God said, "Remember the Sabbath day by keeping it holy" (Exodus 20:8), they will be closed on Sunday. This allows their employees to obey the fourth commandment. Are you kidding me? Do you know how hard it is to make money in the retail business? You have to work and scrape for every nickel. How could you close on Sunday when the competition does not? But these two companies are not trying to obey the competition. They are trying to obey God. They believe strongly that the way that they are to obey God is to close on Sunday.

So they do it. Their employees see these companies modeling, "Love and obey God." What about their customers?
My family has accidentally pulled into a Chick-fil-A only to
realize that it is Sunday. Even though I couldn't get one of
those great sandwiches, I am thankful for that company. I
will come back on Monday.

Recently, I saw a special on one of the television networks about Chick-fil-A and their president, Dan Cathy.
The interviewer was practically spellbound at the story of
this company. How could the company keep up with other
restaurants when they close on Sunday? Mr. Cathy related
that instead of losing revenue by closing on Sunday, they
make more than their competition. Their loyal customers
just eat there on the other six days and wind up spending as
much money as they would have on Sunday. They appreciate (or at least understand) the commitment that the company makes. God blesses the company with a great product
for which there is such a demand. The Sunday closing does
not disturb its competitiveness in the market.

As each new store celebrates its grand opening, the first
one hundred customers receive a free meal each week for
the first year. In order to be in the first hundred, customers
camp out. The stores create activities to help pass the time.
It becomes a giant party. Even Dan Cathy camps out with
them. He meets customers. He shares his story. He prays
publicly and offers thanks to God for food and for the store.
Now that's discipleship! No one can question about whom
Chick-fil-A is serving or where it stands in its faith. It is obvious to all. *As you go . . .*

A friend of mine, George, took "as you go" seriously a number of years ago as he helped John Tolson start The Gathering of Men ministry in the early 1980's.[3] When John was an associate pastor, he met George at his church. John offered to meet with George for an hour each week. The two studied through the Gospel of John. Little by little, George began to understand the truth about Jesus Christ and committed his life to Him.

At about the same time, John saw the need for a men's ministry in Houston, but he needed a place to meet. George offered the lunch area and auditorium of his office building for John's meetings. Men like Tony Campolo came to Houston to share the gospel. Many men were changed because of John's vision and George's generosity with his building. George helped in inviting businessmen around Houston and many came because of his involvement.

Thirty years later, George is still participating in discipleship and, according to him, he is doing more than he ever dreamed he would. The vital ministry he helped start is now in ten cities across the country with additional cities coming on board. God has used these two men to share the gospel with literally tens of thousands of men. *As you go . . .*

Remember the story of Paul and Mark? In Acts 12:25, Paul and Barnabas were returning from one of their mission trips and decided to take John Mark with them. In Acts 13:13, we read that Mark left them and returned to

---

[3] You will hear more about The Gathering of Men in "A Contemporary Application" in the back of the book.

Jerusalem. Commentaries point out that Mark got home-sick or frightened or somehow lost his desire to be on the trip. For whatever cause, Mark deserted Paul and Barnabas and went home. It should be noted that it was during this trip that the two older men endured much hardship, and it was at this time that Paul was stoned within an inch of his life (Acts 14:19).

End of story? Not quite. When the time came for the next trip, Barnabas suggested that they get Mark and take him (Acts 15:37–41). Paul was totally against it because Mark had already deserted them once. The Bible says that the dispute was so bad that Paul and Barnabas split up with Paul taking Silas and Barnabas taking Mark.

What does this have to do with discipleship?

We do not have a record of the trip that Barnabas took with Mark, but we do have an idea as to what happened. Much later, as Paul wrote to the churches that he had established, he mentioned Mark on a couple of occasions. In his letter to the Colossians, he said, "My fellow prisoner Aristarchus sends you his greetings, as does Mark, the cousin of Barnabas" (Colossians 4:10). Paul was now under house arrest at Rome and Mark was with him! Paul later wrote Timothy from his final prison cell and said, "Only Luke is with me. Get Mark and bring him with you, because he is helpful to me in my ministry" (2 Timothy 4:11).

What happened between Paul and Mark?

I think that both of these men changed due to the discipling heart of Barnabas. Barnabas took Mark on the mission trip with him and I imagine as they travelled he carefully taught Mark. I am sure that Mark was greatly impacted by the faithfulness of his older friend. However it happened, Mark must have changed into the person that Paul wanted. And I think that Paul might have changed as well, again under the tutelage of Barnabas. Paul probably learned a lesson on forgiveness. Maybe, through Barnabas, he came to better understand the message of grace that Christ imparted on the cross. Both men were transformed to be closer to the character of Christ because Barnabas worked with them as he went on his mission trip. *As you go . . .*

Or what about when Paul was in prison and wrote the letter to the church in Philippi? Can you imagine what it would be like to be separated from a ministry and thrown into jail? There are Christians throughout the world who know what this is like. In America . . . not so much. Paul was incarcerated for his faith and could only write the Philippians a letter rather than visiting them in person. To most of us, it would look like his ministry was over. As it turns out, it was just beginning. His letter to the Philippians is one of the most optimistic and joyful books in the Bible. Some of us would be asking people to pray for our release or we would be feeling sorry for ourselves. Not Paul. Listen to what he says as he writes to his friends:

> Now I want you to know, brothers, that what has happened to me has really served to advance the gospel. As a result, it has become clear throughout the whole palace guard and to everyone else that I am in chains for Christ.
>
> —PHILIPPIANS 1:12–13

Paul was not concerned about his life. He was too busy trying to share Christ with the prison guards! He trusted God for his current circumstances and took advantage of the time that he had with the men who were sent to guard him. Instead of Paul being chained to the guards, the guards found that they were chained to him. They probably had to listen to the gospel all day long. Those conversations must have been amazing. Paul says in Philippians 1:12–13 that his imprisonment advanced the gospel. The prison guards were changed because Paul was there. He made disciples in the worst of circumstances. He experienced this achievement for the Kingdom when all looked dark. How do we know that he was successful? As he closes the book of Philippians, he says, "Greet all the saints in Christ Jesus. The brothers who are with me send greetings. All the saints send you greetings, especially those who belong to Caesar's household" (Philippians 4:21–22). After Paul departed prison, he left disciples within the court of Caesar. He had made a great impact in a godless world. *As you go . . .*

WHO ARE YOU impacting "as *you go*"? Is someone being transformed because of your obedience to Christ? Most of us are leading someone; we just don't know who it is and where we are leading them. Here's a good question to ask yourself: "If someone followed me, where would they end up?" We are all leaders of some sort. Our followers will end up where we are going. Christ calls us to be ones who lead others toward Him. Are you doing it?

My friend Flip Flippen, in College Station, Texas, runs

one of the world's largest training companies for educators, businesses, and sports organizations. They have prepared thousands of men and women to be better leaders. Flip gave me permission to share with you the four questions that he gives teachers to use with students who are not behaving appropriately or not following instructions. While these questions are designed for a classroom of young people or for a child at home, they also work in the "classroom" of life for adults.[4]

The teacher begins by asking, "Sweetie, what are you doing?" Flip actually uses the word, "sweetie." It disarms the conflict that could arise by asking questions that are as convicting as these. This first question is designed to draw the child's attention to what he is doing, right now. The teacher knows that they are not doing what he wants of them, but he wants them to discover it themselves. Instead of beginning the discussion with a confrontation, he merely asks a question.

The second question is this: "What are you supposed to be doing?" The correct answer should be whatever activity or assignment has been given to the child or the class. If the youngster doesn't know, the one doing the teaching can then re-instruct the student as to what he should be doing. Once again, no strong communication is needed. The teacher is simply leading the child to discover the truth about his behavior.

---

[4] The Flippen Group: flippengroup.com.

The third question is, "Are you doing what you are supposed to be doing?" Is the directive being followed? This is always answered with a simple yes or no. There is no other answer that will work. Any attempt to justify current behavior can be met with a repeat of the question, "Are you doing what you are supposed to be doing?"

The final question is, "When would you like to start doing what you are supposed to be doing?" Does the young person have any intention of following orders? Of course, if the child says, "Never," he is indicating that he does not want to be in class and some other measures may be needed. To refuse to do what the instructor deems necessary will either lead to a trip to the principal, a visit with the parents, or another appropriate punishment. Hopefully, the child has been led to see that his current activity is not what his superiors believe is best, and he will alter his behavior.

So let me ask you four questions that Jesus might ask:

1. *"Sweetie, what are you doing?"* What are you doing with your life and faith? What takes up your time? Not very many Christians actually have a plan for their spiritual life and growth. This question may give you a chance to think about what your life communicates about your Christian mission. If someone observed your life, would they be able to understand your calling as a Christian?

2. *"What are you supposed to be doing?"* What is it that Jesus asked you to do? If you are not sure, turn back to Matthew 28:19–20. The Great Commission is not the Great Suggestion. It is the command of Jesus to His disciples. Are you His disciple? If you are following Him, then He is making

that directive to you. You are supposed to be making disciples. Jesus made that very clear, didn't He?

3. *"Are you doing what you are supposed to be doing?"* Well, are you? Look at your average day and see what you find. This is a simple answer. No explanations are necessary. You are either obeying Jesus by doing what He asked you to do, or you are obeying someone else. If you are obeying someone else, could you be considered a follower of Jesus?

4. *"When would you like to start doing what you are supposed to be doing?"* If you are not doing what Jesus asked you to do, what are you communicating to Him about the importance of His commandments to you? How would you answer Jesus if, somehow, He could physically stand in front of you and ask you this question? Scripture is the Living Word of God, and we must believe that through the Bible, God speaks personally to every one of us. So, in reality, Jesus *is* standing in front of us, asking this question.

When are we going to get around to making disciples? It is Jesus' command for us. He was very clear when He gave it. When it comes down to it, we all understand what He meant by what He said.

"When would you like to start doing what you are supposed to be doing?"

Discussion Questions

1. How does the translation of "go" to "as you go" free you to make disciples? Will it make a difference for you?

2. If you were leading a major retail chain, would you close on Sunday? Why or why not?

3. What can a business owner or leader do to honor God and make disciples while continuing to be profitable?

4. Does the story of Barnabas and Mark give you some insight on making disciples? What do you think that it communicated to Mark? What about to Paul?

5. Discuss the four questions from the Flippen Group. How might they apply to your family or to those who work for you? How does it apply to you?

6. How do you answer the question, "When would you like to start doing what you are supposed to be doing?" (As it applies to disciple making.)

Chapter Fifteen

Why Aren't We Doing It?

As long as we play at evangelism, with no risk to our
selves and no price to pay, we shall make little impact
on our society. When we see evangelism, not as a gentle
Sunday sport, but as the serious, costly business of
everyday life, we may have to ride out many storms but
there will be a fishing harvest for God's glory. In some
parts of the world Christians are being urged by church
leaders not to evangelize because, it is said, religious
and political situations are too sensitive. How would
Stephen or Phillip have reacted to that?[1]

—DAVID WATSON

THE GREATEST OBSTACLE we face in discipleship is not
what curriculum to use. Nor is it incredibly difficult to find
someone who wants to be discipled. Furthermore, leadership is not an issue; there are many strong leaders in the
church who could be mentors. No, the greatest hurdle is a
simple matter of obedience. *Will we do what the Word tells
us?* Will we be committed to the process that Jesus left us?

I once spoke at a retreat on this subject, and at one point,
I asked those present if they were making disciples. When
no one indicated that they were, I asked, "So, why do we

---

[1] Watson, p. 147.

think that it is OK to disobey Jesus?" Sometimes, I might get too direct, but that is the question isn't it? Why do we think that it is acceptable to deliberately disobey the direct command of Jesus? Did Jesus ask us to do it? That seems like an easy question to answer. It also would appear that our response to the command should be fairly simple.

Hopefully, you and I are now close enough to be honest. Are you making disciples? Do you have someone who would think of you as his or her mentor? This would be someone for whom you are regularly making time in your schedule and for whom you are interrupting your life. If not, why not? Does God think that it is all right when we do not do what He asks?

There are probably several reasons that we are not making disciples. I want to identify some of those in this chapter. I do not focus on this in order to judge or condemn. No one is obeying the Lord perfectly, certainly not this writer. It would be wrong to simply attempt to point a finger at those who have not reached the place in their life where they are ready to take on a disciple. Hopefully, this chapter, along with the other discussions in this book, will help make you ready. I have picked four reasons why many have been slow to embrace Christ's command. There are probably more, but four will do.

1. We are not being challenged to do so

When was the last time a teacher or pastor openly challenged you to make disciples? That instruction is not so prevalent in the Christian teaching of today. I am not saying that it is completely absent, but there is not a widespread, burning passion being planted amongst us to find someone and impart the notion of loving and obeying Christ. There has got to be a good reason for this. Whatever happened to the quote, "Jesus said it. I believe it. That settles it"? That was a famous bumper sticker in the seventies. Today it might read, "Jesus said it. I believe it. But I'm not sure I am going to do it."

What is the burning desire of many churches today? Please note that I am not posing this question to pastors. I am talking to each and every one of us who attend or lead in the modern church. The most important issue, according to the majority of church members (just go ask them), is to grow the church numerically. When I question members about what "church growth" means, they will answer that it means that we are making the church bigger. If we add to our numbers, our assumption is that we will become better at what we do. When we actually think it through, however, are we merely adding more members so that we can add more members? Are we building *organizations* instead of the Kingdom? What happened to helping members grow in their faith? Shouldn't that be our goal? What if we quit worrying about "the numbers thing" and just dedicate ourselves to each other and how each of us loves and obeys God?

By the way, why do you attend the church that you do? Answers will vary, but here are a few. Each one starts with, "We attend this church because . . ."

- ". . . of its contemporary (or traditional) style of worship."

- ". . . of the youth program and our kids like it."

- ". . . of the teaching and preaching of the pastor."

- ". . . it is close to our neighborhood and our friends go there."

- ". . . we got mad at our last church."

OK, stop. Does anyone attend their church because they are being encouraged to get involved in ministry and discipleship? I know that some do, but I fear that most do not. That's why I attend my church. It gives me a place in which I am being discipled by my friends and its staff, and I am able to participate in ministry, both inside and outside the church walls. It is a community of believers who challenge each other to love and obey God. It is a church that would be difficult to leave, unless God called me to go, because these people are my family. A church is not just a place to go. It is a community in which to live.

There are many churches and Christian organizations that, if they were honest, would say, "Discipleship just does not seem productive as far as our desire to grow and expand." If that were someone's stance, we would have to ask, "But wait. Did Jesus say 'Be productive'? Did Jesus say to go make bigger institutions? Didn't He say to make disciples?"

This is sounding a little judgmental to me, so I know that it must sound that way to you also. Yet, what else can we say? We *must* make disciples because Jesus told us, and our need for growing larger organizations cannot stand in the way of His clear command. We must challenge each other to obey the last directive of Jesus. If you are a pastor or a teacher, you should teach, encourage, cajole, or beg your students to be disciple makers. It is what Jesus wants.

2. We are not sure what we are actually supposed to do in discipleship

What is your goal for your Christian life? What? You aren't sure? But you have been reading about Christ's greatest commands for almost two-thirds of this book! Our goal for our Christian life has got to be to love God with all of our being, and then out of our love to obey Him. We should be praying and asking God to help us with our love and obedience to Him. Paul covers those two objectives in his prayer for the Ephesians. In his letter to them, he says:

> I pray that out of his glorious riches he may strengthen you with power through his Spirit in your inner being, so that Christ may dwell in your hearts through faith. And I pray that you, being rooted and established in love, may have power, together with all the saints, to grasp how wide and long and high and deep is the love of Christ, and to know this love that surpasses knowledge—that you may be filled to the measure of all the fullness of God.
>
> —EPHESIANS 3:16–19

Paul is asking God to empower the Ephesians in order that Christ might live within them because of their faith in Him, as evidenced by their actions. Next he prays that they would understand the greatness of God's love. Therefore, within that prayer is the answer to our goal in discipleship. It is that those whom we disciple would grow in their love of God and their obedience to Him.

We get so worried about what to teach and the correct steps to take that we don't disciple at all. It seems so daunting. Our need for perfection tends to bog us down. We are afraid to step out for fear that it will be the *wrong* step. Actually, our biggest duty is to teach our disciples that God loves them. The main issue is simply how to impart that love. Secondly, we should be teaching that God's commands should be obeyed. You and your disciple could read the Bible together and then determine what the passage calls you both to do. That doesn't seem quite so hard, does it?

I am not saying that curriculum is not important. Certainly it is. There are just so many people searching for the perfect program that they forget to go out and do something! I personally believe that material makes up about 20–30% of the effectiveness of discipleship. (I do not have any numbers to back that up. After being in a discipleship ministry for many years, it is just a personal opinion that I have formed.)

I once led a group through a book that I would call a "grade C book." We spent half of our time criticizing the writing and the other half applying it to our lives! It wasn't well written, yet it impacted us. (That gives me hope for this book!) God really blessed our time. Our heart was to love Him more fully, and as we discussed the issues of our lives, we grew in our faith. Do your best to find the material that will help you talk about God with your discipleship group. Be excellent. Find the best content you can—but don't take three years for the search!

3. Discipleship is hard and uncertain

The above statement is true. The process of discipleship is indeed difficult. It is not easy to find disciples who will stick with you and will persevere in their growth. I have watched as men have tried to start small groups or as they invited one man to meet with them. There have been many slow starts. There have also been plenty of stillbirths. Some of my friends have been turned down. If Jesus wanted us to make disciples, why didn't He make it a little easier? It seems that many people are wary about the invitation to be a disciple.

We have a saying in men's ministry which, though perhaps not entirely accurate, still makes a valid point: Only 50% of the men who say they will attend an event the next day will actually show up; 70% of the men who confirm their attendance the day of the event will attend, and 90% of the men who arrive in the parking lot actually attend the event![2] I could apply this saying to discipleship. Many are invited, a lot say that they are interested, yet amazingly few will actually stay with it.

There are no guarantees. Jesus spent three years with twelve men and look what happened: one of them betrayed Him; nine of them ran when He was arrested; and one of the remaining two denied that he even knew Jesus! What would we think about our ministry if we had similar statistics? Of course, with discipleship it is never as it appears.

---

[2] Thanks to David Todd. David was one of the early leaders of The Gathering of Men ministry.

Once the eleven remaining apostles saw the resurrected Jesus, knew without fail that He was the Son of God, and received the Holy Spirit, they all gave their lives as they followed Him—and we are *all* a result of their obedience.

What put them over the top? First, they knew for sure that Jesus was who He said He was. Secondly, through Jesus, they experienced the love of God firsthand.

Our role as those who disciple others is to help them see what we have seen. We help them to love and obey God for through that, they, too, will become convinced of the Truth. During this process, we might not see any progress on the part of our disciples. At any one point, it might look like we have worked in vain. The night of Jesus' arrest it looked like all of His efforts were wasted, however, the story was not complete at that point. Three days later, the disciples were radically changed. Our job is to trust God and allow our disciples to experience the love of Jesus. The results are up to God.

4. We do not want to

What do you do when someone tells you to do something and you really do not want to? I have a little trick at home. If my wife tells me that she has a chore for me, I just act like I don't hear her. It usually works (of course now it won't since she will read this). We do that with God. Jesus said that we should make disciples and sometimes, we just act like we do not hear Him. We just keep on doing the comfortable things. Of course, everyone does know that Jesus said it, so we need other defenses.

One way to ignore the command is to do other things. When my wife asks me to take out the trash, I can quickly come up with another, equally important task that keeps me from hers. After all, someone has to listen to the weather. And who will read the sports page if I don't? These things are vital! When God commands us, we substitute other activities. We might complain that our need to teach a class keeps me from the commitment to really make disciples. Or we could plan programs for our church and get really involved in the activities of the church. The preparation of the Wednesday night supper could be our talent so we busy ourselves with it and overlook the priority of preparing men and women to serve God's kingdom.

Most of us claim the "busy" card when it comes to discipleship. When asked, "How are you doing with discipleship?" we answer, "I have been very busy. My business is going really well, and I just cannot get away." (Isn't it funny that we thank God for the blessings of a prosperous business, but then blame our disobedience on the very work with which He blessed us? God gave us a vocation that keeps us from obeying Him? Are we sure about that?)

Before we tell Jesus no, we should understand that as Christians, we do not have a life. We gave that away to Him when we committed ourselves to Him. As surely as James, John, Andrew, and Peter threw down their nets to follow Jesus, we are called to put our life aside and go after that life to which Jesus called us. We have no rights. We have no agenda except that of being Jesus' man or woman on earth. How then can we say no to His orders?

The best excuse is, "I don't have the gift of discipleship." How can Jesus expect me to disciple others when I do not possess the ability to do so? I've been working on this one and I noticed something. Jesus did not pass out a spiritual gifts test right before He gave the Great Commission. He gave His apostles a command that He knew they could fulfill. He knew that because He had implanted within them the ability to do it. How can we say that Jesus would not gift us with the talent to obey Him? Part of the excitement in living the Christian life is seeing our hidden gifts appear as we obey God. You *do* have the ability to disciple those to whom God calls you. You just have to find "the whom."

In the end, we do not really mean to say no. We just misunderstand that when we said yes to Jesus, we really were supposed to mean it. We gave our lives to Jesus, not just our spare time. Jesus did not die on the cross just to make us comfortable. He came to call us to participate in His kingdom. This Kingdom is being established on the earth. As Christians, we have been invited to join in. Jesus does not promise us a new house or a brand new pickup truck. He offers us a partnership with Him in order to call others to the Kingdom.

There is little room to argue about this call to disciple. We know what our job is, but many of us have trouble envisioning a life that takes seriously this call to the growth of others. We are not sure how we get started and where we should end up. Where do we find a good candidate to disciple? What do we do with them? What should they be doing when we finish? These questions can only be answered by God. We must learn, therefore, to take them to God and look to Him for answers. In the next chapter, we will discuss how to do that.

Discussion Questions

1. Discuss the first paragraph in the chapter. Paraphrased, it says, "The greatest obstacle to discipleship is our decision to do it." Do you agree or disagree?

2. Have you personally ever tried to disciple or mentor someone? What happened? Would you ever try again?

3. What excuses do most Christians use to not disciple? There are several.

4. Why do you attend your church? How could your church offer more opportunities for discipleship?

5. Grade your church, on a 1 to 10 scale, on discipleship. If the grade is high, what is happening to make it so? If it is low, what could you do to change it?

Chapter Sixteen

"God, Give Me Someone to Disciple"

Then he said to them, "Suppose one of you has a friend, and he goes to him at midnight and says, 'Friend, lend me three loaves of bread, because a friend of mine on a journey has come to me, and I have nothing to set before him.'

"Then the one inside answers, 'Don't bother me. The door is already locked, and my children are with me in bed. I can't get up and give you anything.' I tell you, though he will not get up and give him the bread because he is his friend, yet because of the man's boldness he will get up and give him as much as he needs.

"So I say to you: Ask and it will be given to you; seek and you will find; knock and the door will be opened to you. For everyone who asks receives; he who seeks finds; and to him who knocks, the door will be opened.

"Which of you fathers, if your son asks for a fish, will give him a snake instead? Or if he asks for an egg, will give him a scorpion? If you then, though you are evil, know how to give good gifts to your children, how much more will your Father in heaven give the Holy Spirit to those who ask him!"

—LUKE 11:5–13

LET'S SAY THAT you have made it this far because you really believe that it is God's will that you make disciples. After all, Jesus did say it. I am assuming that Matthew 28 is still in your Bible. Want to check? Go ahead. The rest of us will wait. If it is there, then you are left with two questions of obedience:

- Will I do it?
- Who will be the person(s) I disciple?

Isn't there a loophole in all of this? Aren't there many ways to participate in discipleship? The Bible does not come right out and say that we have to just focus on one person does it? Surely, we cannot say that there is only one way to promote discipleship. Does teaching a Sunday school class count? Jesus taught. What about working in the church nursery? Didn't Jesus love children? Does pastoring a church do the trick? Paul left Timothy in charge of the church in Ephesus. What if I just focus on my family? Isn't it discipleship if I take my family to church and allow them to see me live the Christian life? The answer has got to be yes.

But hang on. Aren't all those questions based on the *minimum* that we can do to get by? How do we observe the models of Jesus, Paul, and Timothy? Yes, Jesus taught the multitudes, but he also had a small class (the twelve disciples). Then he subdivided it into an even tighter group (Peter, James, and John). You might even make the case that Peter was Jesus' special project or that John, the disciple that Jesus loved, was His special disciple. Paul founded churches all over the world, but he also paid special attention to his personal disciple, Timothy. He loved him like a son (2 Timothy 1:2). Because of the time that he put into Timothy, a shy, fearful, weak-stomached young man was transformed into a man of God who was responsible for an entire church in Ephesus.

In Second Timothy, Paul wrote to his young disciple and told him to entrust *his* life and message to faithful men who would in turn trust theirs to others. Verse 2:2 says, "The things you have heard me say in the presence of many witnesses entrust to reliable men who will also be qualified to teach others."

So, Paul told Timothy. Timothy told reliable men. Faithful men told others. There are four levels to Paul's command (Paul, Timothy, reliable men, others). I do not believe that kind of multiplication can happen unless you are deeply involved in someone's life. Maybe you can do it with a small group, but I do not think anyone can achieve that level of discipleship by merely teaching a class—and I teach a class! Obedience to God's command, stated through Paul in 2 Timothy 2:2, takes strong personal relationships. You cannot just "get by" and produce four layers of faithful men or women.

Does this mean that you shouldn't teach a class? Of course it doesn't. But your teaching should lead yourself and those under you to discipleship. Scripture indicates that it should. Our teaching should help others to love and obey God. It should leave students with an enhanced desire to love God. If not, why are we teaching in a church or seminary? Our sermons and lessons should be full of God's love. They ought to utilize examples of those in Scripture who obeyed God. We have to constantly challenge our class members and students to step out in faith and trust a God who loves them whether they succeed or fail.

Notwithstanding what I just said above, we are also called to take a small number of people into a deeper relationship with God. Like Jesus, Paul, and Timothy, we should be looking for someone who needs us to help them grow in Christ. Do not short yourself on this. Personal discipleship can be the source of great joy and satisfaction as you see God work through you in helping others find God. It can also be a great heartache. Remember Judas? Jesus gave him three years of His life and Judas never got it. But Jesus was obedient to the call to Judas and in doing that, pleased God.

THE GREAT PROBLEM we face in discipleship, after we decide that we will do it, is how to locate someone to disciple. There are so many people out there. How do I go about the process of finding someone? Luke records what Jesus did before He picked His small group.

> One of those days Jesus went out to a mountainside to pray, and spent the night praying to God. When morning came, he called his disciples to him and chose twelve of them, whom he also designated apostles: Simon (whom he named Peter), his brother Andrew, James, John, Philip, Bartholomew, Matthew, Thomas, James son of Alphaeus, Simon who was called the Zealot, Judas son of James, and Judas Iscariot, who became a traitor.
>
> —LUKE 6:12–16

Prior to His decision as to whom He would call and spend the rest of His life with, Jesus spent all night praying! His ministry was beginning to develop. He had already invested some amount of time into these men. It appears that calls to Peter, Andrew, James, John, and Matthew were calls to follow Him and they took Him up on that. Jesus had a group of disciples that was forming. Luke 6 says that after He spent the night in prayer, He called the larger group of disciples to Him and from *them* He picked the Twelve whom He called apostles ("apostle" literally means "one sent out"). The twelve apostles were those followers whom Jesus specifically picked to be with Him, and who would eventually be given the task of establishing the Christian church and spreading the news about Jesus. How did Jesus decide on whom to invite into these leadership positions? He spent the whole night praying. He did not take this decision lightly. He knew that He needed to pray about this important decision. We should do the same as we attempt to find Christian leaders into whom we want to pour our lives.

Pray for disciples who will in turn make other disciples. In order to get the four levels of discipleship that Paul talked about in 2 Timothy 2:2, our disciples must want to make disciples of their own. Ask your followers before you start to meet with them if they would be willing to make disciples after you finish teaching them. Pray for leaders and then challenge them boldly.

In Luke 11, Jesus is encouraging His disciples to pray. He has given them the Lord's Prayer and now reminds them of the faithfulness of God. He describes the picture of someone needing help and coming, late at night, to a friend's house, looking for bread. The friend, who is in bed, doesn't want to get up. Who of us hasn't gotten "the call" late at night that requires us to arise and go help a friend?

A number of years ago, Suzie and I went on a three-day outing with some friends to a golf resort. She and I arrived at around 6:00 P.M. and went to dinner with our son, Ryan, who was three at the time. After a nice meal, we came back to our room and put Ryan to bed. Tired from the trip, we went to bed around 10:00 P.M. At about 11:30, I was awakened by a phone call from my friend, Jerry. He told me that he and his wife, Nell, were out on the highway about five miles from the resort and needed me to come get them. Knowing our friends and how they like to joke, I laughed and said, "Right. When did you guys get in?" Jerry told me that he was not kidding and that they were truly out on the highway. Once I determined that they really needed help, I unselfishly suggested that they contact AAA auto services and they could help them. Eventually, as Jerry pleaded, I realized that I was going to have to get up and go get them. I did. And as I recall, Jerry then beat me in golf the next day. He didn't require as much sleep as I did.

Jesus' parable is not too different from my story. The neighbor needed food. He persisted in making his point to his friend who eventually opened the door. Here was Jesus' point. Our heavenly Father, who loves us more than we can fathom, will not turn His back on our prayer. As we ask Him for fish, He will not give us a snake. Our need for bread will not yield a rock from the One who calls us His children. A scorpion will not be substituted for an egg. God knows how to give us great gifts and He will not turn away from those who come to Him for help.

So let's all begin to plead to God for disciples. What will happen if you decide to go to God and ask Him to give you someone whom you can teach about the faith? We should be diligent in our prayer because we believe that God will answer it. If He would generously take care of our need for food, He will also give us help in obeying His command to make disciples. So shouldn't we be asking Him for the ability and the resources to make disciples? Doesn't it make perfect sense for us to ask God for a disciple? It really does.

When was the last time that you prayed and asked God to give you a disciple? If you are anything like me, it has probably been a while. I constantly forget to ask. I start looking around without first requesting that God lead me to the right person. Since discipleship is God's business, we should ask Him who to choose. Since prayer characterized the life of Jesus and since we are trying to follow Him, we should set aside blocks of time to consider whom God would have us disciple. On many occasions, our need to be productive causes us to rush past our prayer time.

It was not very long after the disciples had come to meet Jesus that they realized He was operating under a different priority system than they were. In Mark 1:35–39, we see that Jesus upset the disciples' applecart by being absent from early morning roll call:

> Very early in the morning, while it was still dark, Jesus got up, left the house and went off to a solitary place, where he prayed. Simon and his companions went to

> look for him, and when they found him, they exclaimed: "Everyone is looking for you!"
>
> Jesus replied, "Let us go somewhere else—to the nearby villages—so I can preach there also. That is why I have come." So he traveled throughout Galilee, preaching in their synagogues and driving out demons.

How could Jesus not have gotten the message? Everyone was looking for Him. There were people to be healed. The needs were great. He had to get going! The disciples came to Him and were not too shy about telling Him that He was needed. They were ready for the new day and they knew exactly what had to happen. The only problem (for them) was that Jesus was getting His orders from another Source. He was waiting for God to send Him where He needed to go. When the disciples found Him, He told them that they would be leaving this town and going to new places. They had some traveling to do. You or I would probably have stayed in Capernaum. They were successful there. That was not God's plan, however. Jesus knew because He had spent time with the Father and had listened as He received His next instructions.

Before you rush off to find your first or next disciple, maybe you should get still and listen to God. We need to become men and women of faith who look for God's leading. While we actually *want* to become people of certainty or success, we *need* to become those who trust God. In order to find God's true will for our lives, we must get quiet before Him and allow Him to tell us where we should go next and with whom we should spend time.

As we pray, we can listen to our Creator as He gives us the reason that He created each of us. We were made to know Him. We were made to follow Christ as He establishes the kingdom of God on the earth. We were made to make disciples just as He commanded us the day He left earth. As we embark on this task of discipleship, let us commit to be men and women of prayer. Let us start with this:

"Lord, I pray that I would be relentlessly plagued by the desire to make disciples. Please do not let me settle for less than what You want for me. Give me endurance to stay the course; to find the right person and to stick with the person that you give me until they are, in turn, able to go find their person.

"God, give me someone to disciple."

Discussion Questions

1. What are the great prayer needs for the Christians that you know? What are yours? What if you put the three prayers from this book first? What would that do to the other prayer needs? (Hint: It might NOT take them away.)

2. Do you think that teaching a Sunday school class constitutes discipleship? Why or why not?

3. Do the pastors and ministry leaders you know take an active and personal role in discipleship? For those who don't, what reason do you think they might give for not participating?

4. What do you think would happen if someone began to dedicate more time to prayer and listening to God? Why don't we do it?

5. We all will either spend an eternity with God or without God. What, then, should we be doing with the short time that we are given on earth?

Chapter Seventeen

The Result of Making Disciples

It was he who gave some to be apostles, some to be prophets, some to be evangelists, and some to be pastors and teachers, to prepare God's people for works of service, so that the body of Christ may be built up until we all reach unity in the faith and in the knowledge of the Son of God and become mature, attaining to the whole measure of the fullness of Christ.

Then we will no longer be infants, tossed back and forth by the waves, and blown here and there by every wind of teaching and by the cunning and craftiness of men in their deceitful scheming. Instead, speaking the truth in love, we will in all things grow up into him who is the Head, that is, Christ. From him the whole body, joined and held together by every supporting ligament, grows and builds itself up in love, as each part does its work.

—EPHESIANS 4:11–16

IF YOU PRAYED, "God, give me someone to disciple," what can you expect? Will life change immediately and will you have scores of potential disciples calling your home and asking for you to rush over? I kind of doubt it.

If you were on your way to the hardware store to buy an answering machine to hook up to your new phone number, 1-800-DIS-CIPL, maybe you should wait. It might be a little more complicated than that.

Those who have gone down this road have discovered

that it is a difficult one. Folks who are interested in being
committed disciples are sometimes hard to find. Our prayer
may well ferret out a new pupil quickly, but maybe not. So
if you pray the prayer above, what could happen? I've got
four ideas.

Result #1: You will be changed

First, you will be changed. When you begin to ask God
to make disciples available, He will begin to open your eyes.
That prayer comes from a new awareness of Jesus' Great
Commission and a new desire to be obedient. As you begin to pray, you may find yourself searching. You may start
to consider who may need Him. You might begin to think
about people at the office or at church in a different way. Ask
the following questions: To whom are you naturally drawn?
Who are your acquaintances? Who in your life has asked
you for advice or sought your help? Who likes you? Who
is in your small group? Who plays golf or tennis with you?
With whom do you work or with whom do you work out?
Take notice of people you know. Might they be interested in
having a more mature Christian input to their life?

If you feel like God is saying no to your prayer, recon-
sider your next step. I recently was meeting with a man who
really wanted a disciple, but as he asked several people, they
all turned him down. It was important at this time for him
to realize that they weren't rejecting him; they were just
not ready to concentrate on their spiritual lives. He started
to wonder if he might be better suited for leading a small
group. Since he was interested in inner city ministry, I suggested that he put together a group of folks to learn about

serving in that sector of our community. As of this writing, he does not have a group, but he is praying and believing that God will use him in some real way. The change he is experiencing is that he has a sense that God wants him to pray. He is trusting God for the results. He is maturing in his faith as he loves and obeys the Lord in new ways.

If you are not presently ready to lead someone, God may stop you from finding a disciple. Before you stop looking, talk to a friend who knows you, and ask if he or she believes that you are prepared to disciple someone. Remember, you are only looking for someone who is less mature than you are in the faith. Unless you are the very last in the maturity line, there should be someone with whom to work. It is possible, however, that God may want to teach you something first. Be ready for that. If you are slow in finding someone, change your prayer. Ask God to lead you in the right direction in disciple making. Pray that God would give *you* someone to lead *you* as you try to grow. Maybe you need a discipler first in order to prepare you to make disciples. Ask God to put the right teaching, person, or experience in your path in order to make you ready for service.

One word of warning: If you ask God to lead you in the right direction, you had better buckle your seat belt. God is more interested in your growth than your comfort. What would He do to conform you to the image of His Son? Take a look at Romans 8:28–29:

> And we know that in all things God works for the good of those who love him, who have been called according to his purpose. For those God foreknew he also predestined

to be conformed to the likeness of his Son, that he might be the firstborn among many brothers.

He will do whatever it takes! All things work to the good because God is conforming the believer to the image of Jesus Christ. If you desire to be like Jesus and to be obedient to Him, you can expect God to do almost anything in order to facilitate your growth. The road to loving and obeying God goes right through the life of Jesus. You can check out what His life was like. Then you can expect similar experiences.

Result #2: Making disciples will cost you

Secondly, if you want to care for a growing Christian, there is no limit to the time that it might take or the heartache that you may encounter. Don't be surprised when you get stood up for a meeting. People do tend to forget appointments (or at least, the ones whom I meet with do). Your disciple may "better deal" you for a game of golf or a fishing trip. Or he may get called into a business meeting and forget to let you know. He may decide to sleep in instead of honoring a commitment for a breakfast with you. You can expect to be forgotten, rejected, or slighted. That is exactly what happened to Jesus.

Brace yourself to learn more about your disciple than you want to know. This person may have the worst husband or wife, the most rebellious children, and the hardest financial situation that you have ever encountered. You may feel totally unprepared for the kinds of conversations in which you will participate. It would take a double PhD in psychology to straighten out this person. How are you going to do it? Remember that you prayed about this. God has appointed you to care for this person. You are exactly the right person for the task. If all things work for the good for those who are being conformed to the image of Christ, then both you and your disciple are included. Your relationship will change you both—for the good—because God is in charge.

So about this time, you are maybe thinking that you won't ask for a disciple. Maybe you should settle for a puppy. Maybe Jesus did not mean to apply His command in Matthew 28 to you. Why sign up for this chaos? You do it because you want to love God. You are acting in obedience. Hopefully, you want a life that is nothing short of following Jesus in all that you do. Nobody said anything about convenience or ease. Discipleship can be difficult, but it is absolutely the best way to impact the lives of those who will agree to your mentorship. There is no substitute for the impact that one life can have on another.

What if you are not successful in your attempt to disciple this person? In fact, what if you really fail big time? Isn't that God's business? He desires to see faith in the lives of those who follow Him (Hebrews 11:6). You must trust Him for all the results. He hooked you up with this person (you prayed, remember?), and you have to trust in the infinite wisdom of God, instead of your fear and pride. God is doing something not only in your disciple's life, but in yours as well. He is not in the business of dropping the ball on those who trust Him. He will not let either of you down. If you both stay after it, you will see how God changes the two of you.

Result #3: Other lives are transformed

There is a third result of your prayer. After all the disappointments and all of the work, something miraculous happens. People's lives are actually transformed. I did not say that you would always *see* this change. Sometimes, you won't. Yet, after years of working with people, you may begin to experience some results. (Yes, I said, "years.") Those who have made it a lifetime discipline of making disciples find that they will soon have a string of folks whose lives have been dramatically altered for Christ. Who will choose a lifetime of disciple making? Almost anyone who does it once will wind up doing it again. It becomes habit forming. You come to understand that obeying Jesus is great fun and greatly rewarding. The blessing is that you see your life being used for the kingdom of God.

Ask anyone who has ever worked in Young Life or in a youth group. They have disciples who are now adults, running around all over the country. I was a Young Life leader, as a volunteer and on staff, for thirteen years. I have Young Life kids everywhere. One of them is on television in Houston every night as a sportscaster. He is now a vital part of our community. And we were able to play a small part in his spiritual growth. I have an old Young Life "kid" who is now my doctor. One of my former kids majored in engineering at college and went on to help design the Stealth Bomber. (We almost "killed" him on a retreat for misbehaving. Luckily, we changed our minds—we may have helped our country to win wars by not ending that kid's life that weekend!)

Many teenagers with whom we spent time are now,

themselves, leading teenagers. A while back, I spoke at a banquet at which *my* former Young Life leader, Harry, was present. Also, one of my former students, Amy, was there with her current disciple, Anne. There were four generations of discipleship right there before us (Harry, Roger, Amy, Anne)! A number of years ago, one of the full-time Young Life staffers in Houston approached me. He said, "Do you remember speaking on a retreat in 1981 at Lake Conroe (near Houston)? I became a Christian at that time. I am here because you took the time to share the gospel with me." What an inspiration!

It doesn't just work with kids. I have adults who have come through our men's ministry whose lives have changed because of God's presence in their lives. There are men who had never done anything in Christian leadership until they started attending a small group or Bible study. Due to the commitment of their leader, great things have happened. I know of several men who are now leading groups themselves because of what they learned from another man. Once, I was meeting weekly with a guy in a one-on-one format. We spent an hour each week together before we went to work. I was not too impressed with what we were doing, and I even wondered if I was wasting both of our time. One day, his wife came up and thanked me. She said that she could see a difference in his life. Unbelievable! This stuff really works.

I know what you may be thinking. In the stories above, it sounds like I am "tooting my own horn." *Look at all I have done. I am really something.* That is not the case. On a scale of one to ten on the leadership scale, I am probably about a six or seven. I do some things right. I fail miserably and often at others. I just try to be obedient. God, from time to time, allows me to see how *He* worked through my efforts. My illustrations are there to help you to see how God might use you. The longer that you are on the discipleship trail, the more stories that you may accumulate. Your life can then be an encouragement for others. So get going and stay with it! Great things will happen.

Result #4: We better understand Christ

Here is the fourth and final blessing of praying that God would give us a disciple. We come to better understand the servanthood of Christ. In John 13, Jesus brought the disciples together for their last supper together. During that time, He illustrated to them what real servanthood would look like among them. Take a look at the passage below:

> The evening meal was being served, and the devil had already prompted Judas Iscariot, son of Simon, to betray Jesus. Jesus knew that the Father had put all things under his power, and that he had come from God and was returning to God; so he got up from the meal, took off his outer clothing, and wrapped a towel around his waist. After that, he poured water into a basin and began to wash his disciples' feet, drying them with the towel that was wrapped around him.
>
> He came to Simon Peter, who said to him, "Lord, are you going to wash my feet?"
>
> Jesus replied, "You do not realize now what I am doing, but later you will understand."
>
> "No," said Peter, "you shall never wash my feet."

Jesus answered, "Unless I wash you, you have no part with me."

"Then, Lord," Simon Peter replied, "not just my feet but my hands and my head as well!"

Jesus answered, "A person who has had a bath needs only to wash his feet; his whole body is clean. And you are clean, though not every one of you." For he knew who was going to betray him, and that was why he said not every one was clean.

When he had finished washing their feet, he put on his clothes and returned to his place. "Do you understand what I have done for you?" he asked them. "You call me 'Teacher' and 'Lord,' and rightly so, for that is what I am. Now that I, your Lord and Teacher, have washed your feet, you also should wash one another's feet. I have set you an example that you should do as I have done for you. I tell you the truth, no servant is greater than his master, nor is a messenger greater than the one who sent him. Now that you know these things, you will be blessed if you do them."

—JOHN 13:2–17

All of the disciples are sitting there and are looking around for the servant who would wash their feet. There was none. It probably never crossed their mind that one of them should do it. Jesus stood up and prepared Himself for the job. The men must have shifted uncomfortably as He made His way around the circle. When He came to Peter, he protested and told Jesus that He should not wash his feet.

Why did Peter say that? It is probably because he himself would never do it. Peter may have been saying, "Jesus, we don't want you to do what we ourselves are unwilling to do." After He went around the circle, Jesus sat back down and explained His actions. He reminded them of something that He had told them on several occasions. In order to be His disciples, they must learn to serve each other. He was setting an example for them to follow. Since they were not greater than He, they should have expected to serve each other. The problem was that they, in fact, thought of themselves greater than that. They needed this point to be pounded home. To follow Jesus was to be a servant to all of those who God would bring their way.

We forget that truth sometimes . . . OK, most of the time. The idea of discipleship may bring it to the forefront. We envision ourselves as too important to devote time to just one person or a small group. When Jesus reminds us about it, we protest just like the first disciples. Jesus cannot mean that we should be saddled with the prospect of caring for some other believer. How could that be correct? Some of you lead giant corporations. Others lead churches and ministries. The people who have those responsibilities have very little time. Shouldn't we be focusing on "greater" activities? We live in a world of multiplication. The idea of investing our lives into just one person doesn't seem like a good payoff.

It is important to note where Jesus spent His time. He taught large crowds sometimes, but He also ate dinner with Zacchaeus (Luke 19). He sat down one afternoon with a woman while she drew water (John 4). He was willing to meet late at night with Nicodemus (John 3). He let children climb all over Him (Mark 10). He touched lepers (Matthew

8) and healed several blind men (Mark 8, 10, and John 9, just to mention three). None of these people were the kind to whom any of us would be naturally drawn. Most were not influential people. There was no evidence of payback to this investment of time. If we are interested in following Him, we must do the things that He would do and spend time with whomever He puts in our path. A great part of our blessing will be discovered as we become like Him, doing in imperfect ways what He would do. He speaks through us and encourages through us. We cannot take the credit, but we get to be there when the miracles happen. The world might not approve, and there may even be other Christians who tell you that you are wasting your time. But I think Jesus is honored as we seek to obey Him.

DISCIPLESHIP. IT CAN happen to you. God will bless your efforts as you try to teach and inspire others. We are so sure that we do not have the ability to lead someone closer to Christ. Yet it is really Christ who does the leading. We are just along for the ride. You do not have to be a seminary graduate; you just have to be willing to give away a little time and energy. People will be blessed because of you. People will be in heaven because of what God does through you. No fooling.

Please begin to commit to pray for someone to enter into your life. It is God's way to build His kingdom. He does it one person at a time. I know that we want to influence whole football stadiums at one time, but I believe He does it mostly through relationships of a few folks who get together and talk about their life with God. Our greatest accomplishment may be in the life of just one person. Take a chance on the Creator of the world and make the commitment He leads you to make.

Discussion Questions

1. If God can do all things, then He certainly could bring people to Himself without us. Why does He use us? What do you get out of discipling another Christian?

2. If someone begins to pray for a disciple and cannot find one, what should they do?

3. In your opinion, what is the greatest blessing that one can experience while making disciples?

4. If you had been at the Last Supper and no one washed feet, what would you have done? What would you have said or done when Jesus began to do it?

5. Why should you not try to disciple someone? What gifts do you *not* have that you would need?

6. Will you make the commitment to ask God for a disciple? When will you start praying that prayer? (Like *exactly* when and where?)

Chapter Eighteen

The Smile of Jesus

"Well done, my good and faithful servant."
—MATTHEW 25:21

ONE OF THE great pleasures of life comes when my boys do what I ask them. Whether it is to take out the trash or to do their homework or to treat each other with respect, they honor me when they do what I ask them. Their obedience gives me pleasure. I do not like it merely because I get my way. I appreciate their actions because they think enough of me to listen to what I say and then do it. I still love them like crazy when they disobey me, but I am pleased when they obey me. My boys make me smile.

What makes Jesus smile? It has to be the things that please Him. Jesus knows how hard your life is. He knows what it is like to live in a difficult and sinful world.

Jesus will smile when He sees your obedience.

The whole purpose of the cross is that Jesus desires for us to follow Him into a life of servanthood and sacrifice like His. He calls us to live like He lived, and He then extends to us His forgiving grace when we fail.

When I worked in the corporate world, there were times when my boss went away. I would be left with a set of instructions. Depending on how long he or she was gone, I would usually put off working on the hard stuff. After all, it seemed like it would be a long while before he got back and checked up on me. As time drew near for the return, I got going on the project with which I had been left. When it came time for that delightful day when my boss reappeared, the first question I would be asked was, "How did you do on the project that I left?" (Note to those who have a boss: You want to be able to say that you got something done!)

"Yes, I have finished the project and here it is. I couldn't wait until you got back!" Such an answer will possibly reward the employee with a smile and a "Well done" from the boss. At the very least it might illicit a "Hrrumph, let's see it."

NOT TOO MANY years ago, Suzie and I attended a conference in Orlando. On an afternoon off, we decided to visit Epcot. (Secretly, I wanted to go to the Magic Kingdom, but as a "mature" adult, I agreed to go to Epcot. It turned out to be a fantastic experience.) Toward the end of the day, I found myself sitting alone on a bench while Suzie went to buy some coffee for us. All of a sudden, who should walk up and begin to greet people? It was Mickey Mouse himself. There he was! Red jacket, white pants, and a black bow tie. Folks began to flock to him. A line formed as people waited to get their pictures made with Mickey. Little children ran up to him and threw themselves into his arms. Adults— grown adults—walked up and embraced this mouse! It was an interesting moment as men, women, and children alike all recognized the "friend" each of them had grown to love over the years. They had seen him on television, read his comic books, and dreamed about the day they would get to see him. Now they were finally getting their chance.

As I watched, I began to tear up. I realized that when we go home to heaven, our meeting with Jesus may be somewhat like that, though much greater. At Epcot, there were not any feelings of uncertainty, regret, or fear. People just wanted to get near their lifelong friend and have their picture made. There was not any doubt that they recognized Mickey Mouse.

There will not be any question on that day when we get to meet our lifelong Friend and Lord, Jesus Christ, face to face. Years of following Him and obeying Him and loving Him will culminate as we see Him for the first time. Those who have followed Him will flock to embrace and touch Him for the first time. What a day that will be!

Shouldn't it be our goal to prepare for that day when we will face Jesus? What would please Him and cause Him to say, "Well done, good and faithful servant?"

Scripture underscores the importance of faith. Hebrews 11:6 reminds us that "Without faith it is impossible to please God, because anyone who comes to him must believe that he exists and that he rewards those who earnestly seek him."

We have already discovered that faith only exists in obedience. As we obey God, we test our faith in Him. I will not obey someone in whom I have no faith. So when I meet Jesus, what if He asks me, "Did you obey me?" I want to be able to tell Him that, as best I could, I did. Obviously, I cannot obey perfectly, but I want that goal to be my heart's desire. I want to obey Him. I want to *want* to obey Him (this is not a "typo"). Even if I do not presently want to obey, I ask

Him for the desire to do so. I pray and seek and ask. And I believe God will answer that prayer.

One day you will come face to face with Jesus. I know that He won't "hrrumph" your earthly efforts. He might, however, ask you how you did on that discipleship thing. Maybe that will cause you to stammer, and maybe you will mention that you were really busy. The family He blessed you with took quite a bit of attention. Work took up more time than you wanted. But, maybe, just maybe, you will be able to say, "Well, there was this one guy I hung out with and tried to help in his faith . . . It looked like he grew, and at one point he even told me that he had a disciple who seemed to grow."

What will Jesus do if you say that?

I think that He will smile.

It may be a huge smile, maybe followed by a loud laugh as you stammer to justify your existence with a couple of weak examples.

Then Jesus may put His arm around you and lead you through Heaven and say, "One person? Let me show you what I accomplished through you during your lifetime." (Now please note that I am making this up. I really don't know what Jesus will say to you that day.)

Jesus and you walk through the lobby of heaven and out onto the veranda. (Once again, I am not completely sure that heaven has a lobby or a veranda.) There below you is gathered a huge mass of people just waiting for you to arrive. Some of the people you know, most of them you have never seen before. Through heaven's eyes, you understand that although your results seemed small to you on earth, they were just the opposite in view of the Kingdom.

That one guy that you spent time with did indeed devote some hours to another man. The other man, in turn, spent his whole life discipling others, telling them many things that you had told your one guy. One of his disciples—your spiritual great-grandchild, as it were—went overseas, and because of his discipleship, thousands of other men and women began to make disciples. These are men and women whom you never laid eyes upon, yet they were given the same lessons and examples that you gave your one guy. And they are all there on that day as you stand with Jesus. You look at Him and He gives you a huge smile and says, "Well done, my good and faithful servant" (Matthew 25:21).

IF YOU HAVE small children, chances are I know what is decorating the front of your refrigerator. Most likely, it is full of crayon pictures that are not very good. When our boys were three or four, they were not exactly cranking out Rembrandts at school. We had horses that looked a little like hippos with toothpicks for legs. We had portraits of me where my hair only covered the very top of my head, my ears resembled those of an elephant, and somehow, my arms had grown right out of my neck! Why did we keep these "art" projects? It was because our children handcrafted each one just for us. We were proud of them because our boys worked on them with us in mind. We knew their motivation. They wanted to create just the right piece of art that would make us smile.

What does God's refrigerator in heaven look like? Is it not covered with all of our little efforts—efforts that may not look like much to most people, but to our Father, they are treasures of art? We obey God because we have Him in mind. We want to please Him. We want to make Him smile.

Do not worry about outcomes! God will empower us to reap the exact results He desires for us and for those whom we disciple. He is our Father who we can trust because He is loving, righteous, and good. We serve Him and ask Him to use our efforts. We also trust Him to be pleased with us when we obey. Remember, He loves us all the time. Yet, our obedience gives Him pleasure. He is proud of even our roughest "works of art," our steps of faith.

If you have failed up to this point in your life, you can be sure of two things. One is that your best work is probably ahead of you. Begin to ask God today to change you. Ask Him to transform your heart to love Him like you never thought was possible. Maybe you have not prayed that prayer. Jesus will forgive you for not loving Him and will empower you to move toward doing so. Second, you should ask Him for a heart of obedience. As your heart is recreated through the work of the Holy Spirit, you will find yourself studying Scripture in order to do what it says. You will not be successful all the time. In fact, you may fail more than you succeed. Once again, the grace of God is there to clear the slate, day after day, and you get a fresh start.

As you look for commands to obey, you will find yourself face to face with Matthew 28:19–20. Something inside you will cause you to pray, "God, give me someone to disciple." You may fail or succeed (by earthly measures) with what God gives you, but I can promise that the heart of faith that prays that prayer will please God. That pleasure will be shown to us in a smile. The smile of Jesus. When you see it, all other rewards and goals will fade. The smile of Jesus will melt all earthly successes in an instant. It is the smile of Jesus we should seek. It is the one thing that is lasting; in fact, it is eternal.

Discussion Questions

1. What would you like to hear Jesus say to you when you go to meet Him after your life on earth? How could that desire change your current behavior?

2. What activity would you give up once a week in order to spend more time with someone as you teach him or her about following Jesus?

3. When you help someone at work, play, or in the faith, how do you feel? Describe how it might feel to participate with God as someone comes to love and obey Him in a greater way.

4. What would please God about your life? After your answer, look at Hebrews 11:6. Now what would you say would please God? How can you take the steps in your life to please God?

5. Who are most of us trying to impress or please? List
    as many kinds of people as you can. Now, make a
    personal list of people whom you want to please.
    What would change if you began to focus more on
    pleasing God?

Chapter Nineteen

Now It's Up to You

"You yourselves have seen everything the LORD your God has done to all these nations for your sake; it was the LORD your God who fought for you. Remember how I have allotted as an inheritance for your tribes all the land of the nations that remain—the nations I conquered—between the Jordan and the Great Sea in the west. The LORD your God himself will drive them out of your way. He will push them out before you, and you will take possession of their land, as the LORD your God promised you.

"Be very strong; be careful to obey all that is written in the Book of the Law of Moses, without turning aside to the right or to the left. Do not associate with these nations that remain among you; do not invoke the names of their gods or swear by them. You must not serve them or bow down to them. But you are to hold fast to the LORD your God, as you have until now.

"The LORD has driven out before you great and powerful nations; to this day no one has been able to withstand you. One of you routs a thousand, because the LORD your God fights for you, just as he promised. So be very careful to love the LORD your God."

—JOSHUA 23:3–11

THREE SIMPLE MANDATES. Three simple prayers. Each of these will change your life. There is no question about it. The only question is whether you will embrace the call of Jesus to participate with Him in His Kingdom.

We will end in a place that is very similar to where

Joshua left his people. He had led them in their fight as they claimed their "lot" from God; now, with most of the work done, it was time for Joshua to leave them. He simply asked them to remember what God had done for them (v. 3). They had experienced the power of God in all that He had done to their enemies. They had a great history to fall back on. They had seen God at work. Next Joshua called on them to "be very strong" and to "be careful to obey all that is written in the Book of the Law of Moses" (v. 6). Then, in his last thoughts—remember how important last words are—Joshua told his people to obey and love God. He was challenging them to live wholehearted lives. Nothing else would do.

As we conclude, let's return to the LOT acrostic that leads us to love God, obey God, and teach others to love and obey God. These three steps drive us to become wholehearted followers of Jesus. No longer willing to accept cheap and easy substitutes, as we seek our LOT in life, we go after God with our whole being. We will want to experience all that God has for us.

We should first remember the greatest act of God, which was to send His Son to die for our sins. His love for us is everlasting. Secondly, our love for Him should be greater than that which we have for anything in this universe, including our families, our possessions, and ourselves.

Next, we should want to obey Him. Our hearts should be so focused on Him that we long to know Him through our obedience. To do what He commands of us will be one of our greatest roadmaps to the knowledge of Him.

Finally, we should have a great desire to teach others to know, love, and obey God.

Love, Obey, Teach. LOT. It isn't a complicated task, nor, as we have discussed, is it an easy task. It is an eternal job that will lead us to understand Jesus Christ in a great way. It is the heart of discipleship, which is after all, a journey toward Christ-likeness. Here is the summary:

- "Love the Lord your God with all your heart and with all your soul and with all your mind and with all your strength." (Mark 12:30)

- "If you love me, you will obey what I command." (John 14:15)

- "Therefore go and make disciples of all nations, baptizing them in the name of the Father and of the Son and of the Holy Spirit, and teaching them to obey everything I have commanded you." (Matthew 28:19–20)

There are three simple prayers that will point our hearts and minds toward the pursuit of the above mandates. If you forget all that you have read, do not forget these three prayers. The success of this book lies within them:

"God, help me love You more."

"God, help me to obey You."

"God, give me someone to disciple."

These three prayers are the simple application of this book. Whether you agree with all, little, or none of what has been written here, it would be hard to disagree with the goodness of these simple requests. We can all pray these three prayers. We can all find our place in the kingdom of God.

The image of Christ found in Scripture is the bowed head and bended knee as Jesus sought the strength to follow His Father with His whole heart. Will *you* set your heart to pursue His model? I pray that you will.

Discussion Questions

1. What is your greatest "take away" from this book?

2. Have you made any changes in behavior through this reading? What has it been?

3. If you could ask the author one question what would it be? (Now send it in to info@wholeheartedthebook.com.)

4. If you could ask God one question what would it be? (Now send it in to Him by praying about it.)

5. What happens in your life tomorrow now that you have completed this book? Who might be someone with whom you could share your plans or vision? How could you work with someone so that both of you could start loving, obeying, and teaching?

A Contemporary Application

SO ENOUGH OF the theory. How do some of these ideas work in real life? As Christians, we should be asking ourselves how we could encourage those around us to love God and obey Him. How are we really going to do it?

Certainly Jesus would serve as our model for the task of discipling others. As everyone knows, Jesus designed a business plan before He started so that He might have as many conversions as possible. He was careful to measure His success numerically. He did that so that His donors would fully understand the depth and breadth of His ministry. What you might not know is that Jesus founded a ministry called "Disciples For Jesus" and raised about a $2 million annual budget. His staff of 250 (worldwide) became leaders in their field and each prolifically wrote and published a voluminous number of magazine articles and books. They actually founded a magazine, "World Discipleship," and its subscription reached over 375,000, which was an amazing number taking into account that there were no printing presses at the time. The retreat facility, The Judean Transfiguration and Fitness Center, was a blazing success until the founding directors, James and John, entered a heated argument with the board of directors as to who would lead the ministry when Jesus moved on in His work. The ministry hit all-time lows when the board ran out on Jesus during a dispute with government officials. In the end, Jesus was left alone with a soaring budget deficit. There was no one at the helm at the time of His untimely death.

OK, maybe I made all that up. The bottom line is that Jesus didn't do discipleship in the way that we do it today. His focus was much more limited than ours was and His results were infinitely larger. Can you imagine supporting a ministry that year after year had only twelve participants? The "program" that He used appeared to be one of hanging out with a little group of men. He didn't have the six- to eighteenth-month horizon that most of our discipleship programs center around. He did not just carve one hour per week to spend with His disciples. He was with His men almost around the clock, talking to them about His Father. *Jesus' discipleship curriculum was His own life.* His disciples were able to see it happen, up close and personal. They saw Him pray, taking huge amounts of time to seek the will of His Father. They watched Him take time for the least in the world—the children, the poor, and the diseased. He turned their vocational callings into Kingdom work as He asked them to become fishers of men. Jesus allowed His disciples to see Him struggle. He didn't hide His concerns about following the will of God in His own life. Jesus even invited them to spend time with Him on the last night of His life as He talked to His Father about the plans for the end of His earthly life.

Jesus constantly exposed His followers to His vision for them. He called them to the greatest command, that of loving God wholeheartedly. He brought this up every time that He had the chance. If you are a ministry leader, the way to get your followers to buy into your vision is to constantly discuss it in front of them. Teach it, preach it, live it, and ask them to put it into practice in their lives. Do this year in and year out. They will eventually get it. This vision should not be some goal that can be achieved over a period of time, but it should be an overarching truth that shows up in every part of your life and ministry. It is always before you and governs every action that you take.

What follows is a discussion of our attempt to disciple men in Houston. I am sharing our ministry because it is what I know. It may help you think through your own idea of how to take someone who does not know Jesus to a place of active discipleship.

In our ministry, the Houston chapter of The Gathering of Men, the vision is to facilitate the process of discipling men. We have worked hard to make sure that all we do fits into our goal of producing mature followers of Christ. Yes, we know that *we* can never make them mature. That is the sole work of the Holy Spirit. All that we can do is introduce men to Christ, facilitate their growth through learning, and then challenge them to know and obey the teachings of Jesus.

Our ministry plan came from reading several books by Dallas Willard, Bill Hull, Greg Ogden, and George Barna. One of my favorite books on discipleship is Willard's *The Great Omission*. It reminds me what discipleship is supposed to encompass. It is a must read, along with Willard's other works. Bill Hull has also written much in the area of discipleship and I highly recommend his work. His book, *The Complete Book of Discipleship*, summarizes much of his thinking on the subject. In it, Bill divides the process of discipleship with Jesus into several parts.[1] Below, I have detailed how we have folded three of those pieces into our ministry plan.[2] These may be applicable for you personally or for your ministry or church. Ours is not (absolutely not) a "model" ministry. Take our ideas and improve on them, or even throw them out and start all over. Let us know how you did it and then we will copy you!

Come and see (John 1:35-4:46): Evangelism

In this initial step, Jesus' disciples were invited to come and see who Jesus was and what He was doing. We equate this to outreach where we invite men to come and hear about Jesus. We introduce them to Christ and who He is. Evangelism is not a different activity than discipleship; it is a part of it! When someone asks us if our ministry is about evangelism or discipleship, we reply, "Yes!" One must come to acknowledge Jesus as Lord before he can begin to follow Him. The beginning step of any relationship is to meet the person with whom one wishes to have a friendship.

In our ministry to men, we host outreach breakfasts and

---

[1] Hull, pp. 169–185. Note: In order to truly grasp how Bill has summarized discipleship, one should read the book. Bill took his lead from the book by A.B. Bruce, *The Training of the Twelve*. I am only telling you here how we brought Bill's exposition of Scripture into our work.

[2] If you would like to see a picture of our process, go to houstongathering.org and click on "Ministry Strategy."

luncheons, sports events, and business seminars. Each of these is designed to help us meet men around town and then subsequently allow them to be introduced to Jesus Christ. We attempt to make it easy to see what life with Christ is like by letting them hear stories of well-known sports and business leaders. For some of them, it is threatening to attend a church, but in a hotel breakfast or luncheon setting, they can come and hear the story of Jesus without being intimidated. For men, it is much easier to listen to a famous football player or a successful businessman than it is to sit down in a pew and listen to a sermon. Many of them want to run away from anything that would be construed as a sermon! These introductory events may be short but a friendship can be formed in which further sharing can be facilitated. These basic discussions can lead to a man having a real relationship with Christ, leading him to the next step of discipleship.

In addition to getting to know our staff, they are also becoming better friends with the men who bring them. The "table host concept"—where one man hosts a table and brings several of his acquaintances—allows the inviter to forge deeper relationships with the men that he brings to the event. These friendships allow the host to be more open about his faith and give him a chance to discuss it later with his guests.

We will use anything that may help us build friendships with men. In addition to outreach events, we have eaten many meals with men as we attempt to get acquainted with them. We have used "pre-evangelistic" business seminars to help men sharpen leadership or management skills. These allow us to become friends with men who are not even thinking about God.

In your personal life, do whatever it takes to meet those who do not know Christ. Join a health or golf club in order to meet folks from all walks of life. Get involved in Little League, Boy Scouts, or business networking groups. You will meet interesting people who need to know Who you know. All of life should be a "Come and See" step in discipleship. We should be involved in outreach all of the time. Once you have those relationships, share your faith! Do not be afraid to bring it up. Learn a conversational style of sharing the gospel story.[3]

As we share the gospel story, we are inviting others to accept God's forgiveness and to love God because of what God did and is doing. We present a Creator who loves us, and we invite the listener, through the grace and forgiveness of God, to love Him back.

Come and follow (Mark 1:16–18): Growth

After the disciples came to know a little about Jesus, He invited them to follow Him with the promise that He would show them a brand new way to live. He told them how to live in this brand new relationship with their Creator. He taught them how to pray and spent a lot of time telling them about God's kingdom. Sometimes, He shared by

---

[3] One such method is the Bridge Illustration. Go to The Navigators website at navigators.org/us/resources/illustrations/ and pick "The Bridge to Life."

using parables and illustrations. He likened God to the father who waited for his son to return from his rebellious adventure in Luke 15. He might have stopped in the middle of
a walk in order to describe how their relationship with God
was like a vine (John 14 and 15). Jesus told them what God
was like and what they were like. He called them to a new
life in Him with new priorities. Tax collectors invited their
"sinful" friends to meet their new Friend. Fishermen saw
their target change from fish to men.

Some of the men we meet in outreach become followers of Christ. They want to know about this new life. We
use several ways to show them what following Jesus looks
like. Small group Bible studies provide fellowship with other believers and give participants an opportunity to look at
Scripture and think through the implications of following
Jesus. They can ask questions and debate through difficult
issues. The confidentiality of a properly functioning small
group will create a safe place in which one can pose even
the most sensitive questions.

One-on-one relationships are an excellent way to help
others grow with Christ. While it may be one of the most
effective ways, it is avoided by many Christians. As we discussed earlier, the mentor may feel inadequate at the prospect of sitting down and having an open discussion about
the faith with a less mature believer. It is in these relationships, however, that one can be most frank and helpful to
the disciple. In The Gathering of Men, we encourage men
to find another man and begin to meet with him. We often
encourage them to pick a book from a reputable Christian

writer and then discuss the ideas presented in the book. We also use a book called *The Four Priorities* by John Tolson and Larry Kreider. It is a great curriculum that can be used by anyone who wants to disciple others.[4] Originally, I was adamant that the two should always look at Scripture. More recently, I have backed off of that a little. If two men are not familiar with interpreting Scripture, they may begin to have the discussion entitled, "This is what this means to me." Both can become confused. I have many times helped them pick out books with good ideas and let them "duke it out" with the writer. Mainly, I want them to have deep discussions with each other about what a life with Christ means and how they will obey His commands.

We also use testimonies and Bible studies to help men grow. In these formal studies of Scripture, a Christian businessman or teacher will challenge the listener to trust and obey God in his life. By listening to such talks, the less mature believer can be led to grow in his spiritual life.

A huge step in this process is to help the disciple find a local church that he can attend. Many men have grown up with an incorrect view of the church. We need to challenge our disciples to find a Bible-believing community of Jesus followers. We make sure that Christ is being preached and that the church has a process for bringing along new believers before we recommend it. Sometimes our disciples find a church they like so much they no longer need us. If that

---

[4] *The Four Priorities* can be ordered at thegathering.org.

happens, we just go find a new convert and try to stay in contact with the old one!

We must follow the example of Christ as we work with those who are growing in their faith. Jesus did not just call the disciples to be fishers of men and then leave them to figure it out alone. He spent great amounts of time with His followers. He taught, modeled, rebuked, and corrected. He was available to them. He was concerned about their spiritual growth, and He put them in situations that would promote that growth.

The most gratifying and challenging activity in which you can participate is one of leading one or more folks as they learn to love and obey God. There will almost always be someone who could use your help with his or her Christian life. All it generally takes is an invitation from you. It can be as simple as asking someone to read a book with you and then taking some regular time to discuss it. You can meet with a friend or two to discover what they are getting out of their reading. God will bless that activity. Make it a way of life. You will love it.

It is in this stage of discipleship that the disciple is asked to begin to add obedience to his love of God. As a follower of Christ, we search Scripture in order to follow the commands that we read there. This is not just about education. It is about learning from God about what one should do with his new life. The mentor acts as a challenger, encourager, rebuker, and sounding board (see 2 Timothy 3:16–17). The goal is for both the discipler and disciple to become more obedient to God through their relationship with each other.

Come and be with me (Mark 6, Luke 10): Service

After the disciples had been with Jesus for a while, He began to invite them to be with Him in His ministry. He invited them to do what He did and to participate in His work. In Mark 6, Jesus sent out the twelve apostles to go out and heal, preach, and tell people about Him. After one of these trips, Jesus attempted to take the disciples out by themselves for some rest, but people kept following them, making it impossible for them to be alone. Did you ever wonder where all those people came from? I think many of them followed the disciples back in order to find this Jesus they were describing. The disciples had shared about Jesus, and now the people wanted to meet Him.

When they arrived, Jesus had compassion on them (Mark 6:34) and began to teach them. Everyone stayed so long that soon it became time to eat. The disciples went to Jesus and told Him that they should send everyone home because they were hungry. Jesus asked the disciples to feed the people. The disciples remarked that it would take almost an entire year's salary for this meal. The implication was that they were unwilling to spend such an amount. Then Jesus simply asked them what they had. When they replied that they had found one lunch (five loaves and two fish), He instructed them to have everyone get ready to eat! Instead of doing this miracle alone, Jesus recruited the Twelve to be His agents to distribute the food. Why did He do it this way? Maybe it was to allow the Twelve a firsthand experience of "being with Jesus." It was here that the disciples were able to see what Jesus could do with what they had in their hands.

Later, Jesus sent out seventy-two followers (Luke 10). While they were "in the field" (as we say in the ministry world), they preached, healed, and cast out demons. They returned and were blown away with what had happened. I am taking a bit of liberty in paraphrasing their comments from Luke 10:17, "Jesus, you wouldn't believe what happened! Demons submitted to us when we used Your name. This stuff is real!" Jesus sat back and I think that He might have laughed with them as He said, "I saw Satan fall like lightning from the sky!" He was thrilled to use them in defeating Satan as they followed Him in ministry.

In our Houston ministry, we have designed the third portion of our work to call men into service. We first focused on the obvious; training men to be small group leaders and table hosts for our outreach breakfasts. Rapidly, we wanted to do something more than that. We came up with the idea to befriend inner city ministries and planned to send men there to paint, clean, remodel, or perform other manual tasks. Then we discovered something about businessmen in Houston. They don't care much about painting, cleaning, or remodeling. We found instead that they did have huge networks of business colleagues. If we could show them what the ministries needed, they might be able to help us find it. Some saw that the ministries needed computer, accounting, or other business help. They were willing to go to the ministries and provide that type of service. They realized that God had given them many abilities and contacts that could be used for the Kingdom. So began a ministry that would change our lives and many others.

We started to meet with inner city ministry directors to see if we could help them. In an initial meeting with my great friend, Sylvia Bolling of Aldine YOUTH Center,[5] I learned a great lesson. As we visited, I told Sylvia, "I don't know how to help you. I am from a different part of town and I feel like I don't have anything that you need." With great patience and a huge smile, Sylvia said, "Honey, just tell me what you have and I'll tell you how I can use it, because I need *everything*."

Doesn't that sound a little like Jesus asking the disciples what they had when it came time to feed the five thousand?

We found out that "we didn't know what we knew" and "we didn't know what we had."

God began to show businessmen that He had uniquely gifted them to participate in His work on earth. Slowly, we built an organization called The Get Together[6] which in the last eight years has collected over $2 million of "in-kind giving" (items like tables, chairs, sofas, refrigerators, cars, a taco truck, a time clock, temporary buildings, etc.) aiding 25–40 ministries all over the state of Texas, primarily around Houston.

While the amount of goods that has been procured is

---

[5] This ministry in the Aldine area of Houston began in the trunk of Sylvia's car as she tried to help people in her community get in touch with city and government services. The ministry expanded into one that shares the gospel with men, women, and children of all ages. Their website is aldineyouth.org.

[6] The Get Together website is thegettogether.org.

impressive, even more satisfying is the number of businessmen and women who have been involved in ministry. They are plumbers, builders, roofers, contractors, accountants, housewives, pastors, and many more. With two different locations (central and northwest Houston), over 500 men and women have come into some level of relationship with wonderful ministries through The Get Together. They are seeing that they have a place in God's kingdom and are coming to love and obey Him in ways they had never imagined. We have been made acutely aware of the sufficiency of God, as we have seen temporary buildings become resale shops, dirt parking lots become paved, and offices completely resupplied with excellent furnishings that were no longer needed by businesses.

One of the ministries we assisted was helping men overcome the devastating effects of drug addiction. We noticed that the men there were eating beans, with no meat. Subsequently, a Christian man designed a hunting ministry, called Hunters' Harvest.[7] It challenged hunters to turn in meat from hunting trips and, in just over three years, donated over 100,000 pounds! This meat was donated not only to the drug rehab center, but also to ministries all over the city.

A mall in Houston closed its operations, and the owners allowed ministries to wander the deserted halls finding furnishings and leftover products. Approximately $200,000 of

---

[7] Hunters Harvest: huntersharvest.org.

abandoned goods was claimed as valuable assets by ministries. It has been a miracle of discipleship. Men and women have come to love and obey God.

A friend of mine, Ginger, runs Missions Centers of Houston.[8] They care for three communities in Houston and also serve as a training ground for ministry interns that now serve all over the world. She found many parents who, due to a lack of funds, were having trouble celebrating the birthdays of their children. She invented something that she calls "birthday bags." A "birthday bag" is, literally, a birthday party in a bag, complete with a present, cake mix, a pan, candles, frosting, streamers, and any other small item that could be used to create a party. The bag is given to the parents so that they may have the pleasure of giving their children a great birthday. Ginger needed help with the project and began to recruit others to put the bags together. She found my friends Frank and Sandy who took over the project. With their assistance, the program began to grow. Now, hundreds of kids have experienced wonderful birthdays because of Ginger, Frank, and Sandy. At one of the parties, a grandmother offered to let the "birthday boy" decorate his own cake. When she saw what he had written on the cake, she exclaimed, "No, you were supposed to put, 'Happy Birthday' on it." The little boy said, "No, grandmother, I wanted to thank God for my cake, so I wrote, 'Thank You God.'"

---

[8] See the Mission Centers of Houston website, missioncenters.org.

What more could be said? In doing something as simple as putting together a birthday bag, the love of God was displayed. Those who do it are coming closer to God themselves as they attempt to do what Jesus would do if He were physically here today.

Time and time again, Christians find real joy as they do the work of God. Christian theories become life-changing truths when one goes to South America or Africa to help dig a water well.[9] One afternoon given to an inner city ministry in your town can be more relaxing and fulfilling than a day at the golf course or one spent taking a nap. As Christians put on the yoke of Christ (Matthew 11:29), they experience that the weight is indeed light. Life begins to make sense when one sees his or her abilities used by God's people for His work. There are people in your city whom you should meet and with whom you should serve. Life will never be the same.

Discussion Questions

1. What could you do to find a disciple who is not currently a follower of Jesus? How could you bring them to the point to which you could share the gospel?

2. If a new believer asked you to disciple them, where would you start?

---

9 Read about the ministry of Living Water International at water.cc.

3. How could you get a mature believer interested in ministry? Are you familiar with ministries that are in your city?

4. Have you ever been discipled by someone? How might someone find a mentor? What would happen if you asked your pastor to help you?

5. If you were going to design a ministry, inside or outside the local church, that led others to discover and grow in Jesus, what would it look like?

Acknowledgments

THERE ARE MANY people to thank and I am sure that I will miss someone, but I still need to acknowledge all of those who helped me write this book. It is working on something like *Wholehearted* that I most clearly see God's gift of community.

I had many friends who read the manuscript in its early stages. Tony Mayer, Frank Kampe, and Ted Cooper, Jr., were all incredibly helpful and affirming. Wallace Henley at Houston's Second Baptist Church took an entire afternoon to give me many suggestions and much encouragement.

Buck Oliphant read the entire book twice. That was an amazing show of friendship because the early versions were pretty bad.

Jim Rath also read it twice and brought out every dictionary and English handbook that he possessed. I do not think I would have gotten through the process without him. He also thinks that I use the word "that" too much. That is one thing that I do not think that is true, but I appreciate that he told me that. Any remaining grammatical mistakes ain't his.

The idea of "LOT" came from a luncheon with Flip and Susan Flippen in College Station, Texas. When I described the idea of loving God, obeying God, and teaching others to do the same, Susan immediately said, "Oh, that's our lot in life." Susan, Flip, and Lee Bason took a long lunch with me to encourage me to write the book. Sometimes the expectations of our friends serve as our greatest motivation, and they all had great expectations of me. Flip also spent a good hunk of time going over the Four Questions with me that appear in chapter 14.

The major idea of chapter 14 came from a lunch that I had with my friend Paul Gregory. His comments made up the heart of that chapter. Paul feels strongly that "as you go" is an important part of the Great Commission. My conversation with Paul confirmed my idea that I should communicate that fact. And the seafood gumbo was pretty good as well.

My friends Kenny and Craig encouraged me throughout the whole project. Kenny's comments like, "When are you going to finish that book?" kept me going. Wednesday morning drive time with Craig always yields some great conversations and he was always ready to urge me on with the writing.

My advisory board of the Houston Gathering couldn't have been more affirming to the project. Mark, Paul M, Jim S, Glenn, Kenny, Craig, John, Paul O, Robert, Jim R, and Wade kept pushing me to finish the book and were anxious to see it. I do not know who was more excited to get the book, me or Mark Gillespie.

Thanks to Jim Stephenson's small group who tried out the material from the book when it was in its very early stages. Thanks, too, for enduring the many occurrences of the word, *that*.

I owe a huge thanks to John Walker who was incredibly

affirming throughout the book process. God uses him in mighty ways in our ministry. Our periodic seafood lunches are fantastic. I always eat healthy and he always eats the fried seafood platter.

Thanks so much to Tracey, my assistant, and to Dave, my ministry partner. Tracey is a constant help in all that we do in The Gathering of Men. She is also a wonderful editor of letters, memos, AND NOW books! She has been a great friend and help to me for the last seven years. Dave was also a source of encouragement during the work. God has saddled him with trying to keep me in line and I appreciate his semi-success in that area.

My friend and editor and publisher Kit Sublett was my true yokefellow in the book. It was Kit who first encouraged me to write. He was always ready with a joke to break the ice and quick to point out what I had done well. The Lord knows how many passages were not good, but Kit kept working with me to make it readable. Kit is a great friend and a great business partner. My only beef with him is that he stays up later than I do at night and he likes to call me after 10:30. Luckily, we have caller ID . . .

I have an immediate family of four. My oldest son Ryan is 16 and a junior in high school. Chris is 14 and in the eighth grade. Suzie is a chemical engineer and is pretty stinking smart. She is the best wife ever and a wonderful partner in life. And while she is not funnier than I am (even though our friends think that she is), I love her more than anyone on this earth. God has blessed me with the three best people that I could ever live with. I thank them for being patient all the nights that I spent on the phone with Kit and on the computer. I owe all of you some television nights. Thank you for being a great family.

Thank You, Lord, for great friends and family. But most of all, thank You for helping me to love You more and obey You more. Thank You for the gift of discipleship that constantly gnaws away at me and leads me to others. You have given me so many gifts in life, I cannot begin to name them. It truly is a blessing to follow Jesus.

Publisher's Note

Help us discover the result of this book! You can be a part of this story. Send us an email at:

info@wholeheartedthebook.com

Tell us your story. We will post some of them anonymously on the website. Let's begin to talk to each other as we attempt to be the people God called us to be. We can do what He asked us to do, and we can do it in community. Share in the stories of others who are trying to follow Christ. You will be encouraged!

Colophon

WHOLEHEARTED: THREE LIFE-CHANGING COMMANDS OF JESUS
by Roger Wernette

Created using Adobe InDesign CS3 and designed by Randolph
McMann for Whitecaps Media. Original manuscript
prepared in Microsoft Word
Main body composed in Constantia 11 pt., designed by John
Hudson. Titles are composed in Humana Serif Md ITC TT 30
pt., designed by Timothy Donaldson
Cover photograph by Vernon Wiley, istockphoto.com

About the Author

ROGER WERNETTE lives in Houston with his wife Suzie and their sons, Ryan and Chris. Roger was born in Tyler, Texas, and graduated from Stephen F. Austin University with an undergraduate degree in computer science and math; and an MBA. He graduated from Covenant Theological Seminary in St. Louis.

Roger has served as the Executive Director of the Houston chapter of The Gathering of Men since 1998. The ministry seeks to disciple men through outreach, growth opportunities, and service. In 2002, Roger helped to initiate a ministry called The Get Together which organizes businesspeople to volunteer with inner city ministries. He also spent thirteen years on the volunteer and full-time staff of Young Life. Before beginning his service in Young Life, Roger spent eleven years with Pennzoil Company and First City National Bank. In between his time with Young Life and The Gathering, he worked five years in the investment business with Masterson Moreland Sauer & Whisman and Cornerstone Securites. *Wholehearted* is his first book.

Books to help you grow

You might enjoy these other titles from Whitecaps Media

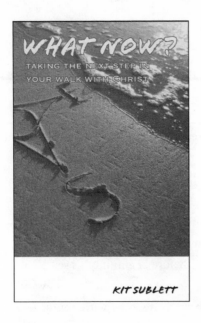

What Now? Taking the Next Step in Your Walk With Christ
124 pages
5.5 x 8.5, paperback

This is the perfect book to give anyone who needs a simple step-by-step guide to taking their faith to the next level. Great for groups.
Study questions available free at whitecapsmedia.com.

Find out how to order these books at whitecapsmedia.com